ENDORSEMENTS

As I travel around the country ministering in revival meetings, I see the power of the Holy Spirit healing people of all manner of sickness and disease—sometimes in unusual ways. Although some do not receive healing instantly, we must still believe Jehovah Rapha can break in at any moment with a miracle. Becky's book *The Healing Creed* helps bolster your faith with key Scriptures and practical insights that inspire a new level of belief in your heart even if the doubt still attacks your mind. I highly recommend adding this book to your library on God's healing power.

JENNIFER LECLAIRE
Senior Editor, *Charisma magazine*
Director, Awakening House of Prayer
Author, *Mornings with the Holy Spirit* and
Developing Faith for the Working of Miracles

Becky Dvorak builds a solid foundation from the Bible for healing in the church. She exposes the enemy's tactics of distracting and robbing the church of the gift of healing through the blood of Jesus. A seasoned prophetic evangelist, you will be encouraged, challenged, and set free from faulty theology that you had no idea you believed in until you read *The Healing Creed*. Becky skillfully leads you into declaring The Healing Creed over your life with Scriptures intertwined with healing testimonies to increase your faith. As a mother of a daughter with special needs, Becky has given me a weapon to wage war for her healing. I encourage you to take this weapon, *The Healing Creed*, in the fight for healing for your friends and family.

LEILANI HAYWOOD
Online Editor of *SpiritLed Woman* and
author of *Ten Keys to Raising Kids That Love God*

The fruit of *The Healing Creed* is this—God's will being established on earth as in Heaven. This is what Becky Dvorak is about—her Father's business. The power of the Lord Jesus manifesting through these pages will change your life! Read it, live it, and be blessed.

WILMER SINGLETON
Founder and President
Voice of the Kingdom E-magazine
The Singleton Publishing Group

The Healing Creed is full of hope, biblical truth, and practical advice. Healing flows from the heart of one who practices what she preaches.

JO ANNE ARNETT
President, Tallahassee Christian College and Training Center

I have found Becky Dvorak to be many things. She is a Christian, wife, mother, grandmother, apostle (translated today as missionary), and dedicated student of the Word of God. I know her to be a genuine follower of Jesus Christ. She stands with the inspired Word as delivered to us by the Holy Spirit. She is a wonderful preacher and teacher.

This most recent written work, *The Healing Creed,* is her best book yet to date. It is thorough, precise, honest, and most of all based solely on Scripture. If you honestly want to know more about healing, how to get it, how to walk it out, how to proclaim it, this book is for you and I believe comes straight from our Father!

I heartily recommend that you get this book and devour it. The Church needs it, individual Christians need it, and this lost and dying world needs the truth contained within these pages.

May the Holy Spirit use this work to bring His people to a closer and more productive place in Him, and Spirit-wrought revival will be the result!

DR. BOB VINEYARD
Senior Pastor, Greenway Spirit and Word Fellowship
Stephens City, Virginia

Those seeking a clearer understanding of healing need to look no further. *The Healing Creed*, Becky Dvorak's newest book, will renew your hope that you can be healed. Becky brings a clear understanding of what the will of the Lord is concerning your health and identifies those things that work against you as well as those things that will increase your faith, enabling you to believe again.

Your faith will be stirred by the teaching and testimonies that Becky shares throughout *The Healing Creed*. We highly endorse this labor of love and would encourage all to read it, especially all our fellow ministers of Christian International Apostolic Network.

Apostle Dr. Jim and Prophetess Connie Childs
Founder-Messengers of Life Ministries, Madisonville, Kentuckey
Author, Conference Speakers, Senior Pastors

A great teacher does more than merely teach truth, they equip students to effectively defend it. In *The Healing Creed*, Becky Dvorak does more than build faith for healing—she keenly exposes the shrewd, unbiblical logic that perpetuates the unjust suffering of so many precious people. In so doing, Becky offers readers the opportunity to think right about God's promise to heal us—spiritually, emotionally, *and physically*—and to secure an unshakable confidence in the loving, healing, and compassionate nature of our Father's heart. I especially loved the insight concerning the believer's dominion over "every living thing" (Chapter 5), which clearly includes the tiny microscopic organisms that create illness. Packed with one real-life testimony after another, Becky Dvorak has given us another significant work that is sure to be a channel of divine deliverance and wholeness for many.

Chad Budlong
Senior Pastor/Conference Speaker
New Foundation Church, Goodyear, Arizona

THE
HEALING
CREED

OTHER DESTINY IMAGE BOOKS BY BECKY DVORAK

Dare to Believe

Greater Than Magic

THE
HEALING
CREED

God's Promises for Your
Healing Breakthrough

✝

becky dvorak

DESTINY IMAGE® PUBLISHERS, INC.

P.O. Box 310, Shippensburg, PA 17257-0310

"Promoting Inspired Lives."

This book and all other Destiny Image and Destiny Image Fiction books are available at Christian bookstores and distributors worldwide.

Cover design by Christian Rafetto

Interior design by Terry Clifton

For more information on foreign distributors, call 717-532-3040.

Reach us on the Internet: www.destinyimage.com.

ISBN 13 TP: 978-0-7684-1099-0

ISBN 13 eBook: 978-0-7684-1100-3

ISBN 13 HC: 978-0-7684-1463-9

ISBN 13 LP: 978-0-7684-1462-2

For Worldwide Distribution, Printed in the U.S.A.

1 2 3 4 5 6 7 8 / 21 20 19 18 17

DEDICATION

The Healing Creed is dedicated to all who seek the truth and the power of supernatural healing that is found in the redemptive blood of Jesus Christ only.

ACKNOWLEDGMENTS

I would like to express my sincere gratitude to Destiny Image Publishers and say a special thanks to the following individuals who helped to bring *The Healing Creed* to you: Larry Sparks (Publisher), Sierra White (Acquisitions Agent/Senior Project Manager/Author Development), Christian Rafetto (cover designer), and John Martin (production project manager). It's a privilege to work with you.

CONTENTS

INTRODUCTION

Do you feel confused about what to believe concerning healing? Many people are unsure these days about what to believe anymore. And rightly so. When we remove the standard of God's Word and teach from human opinion and experience instead of what God says concerning healing, then yes, people will be confused about healing.

But when we choose to make God's Word our standard, we eliminate doubt and confusion and give people a spiritual foundation on which to base their faith, so that they can believe and receive their supernatural healing from the Lord.

We are instructed in Ephesians 6:14 to gird our waist with truth. It is always our responsibility to study the Word of truth and to wrap our lives within it. This will keep the contamination of false doctrine out and the security of God's truth in.

We are to believe in God's message about healing. He asks us in Isaiah 53:1, *"Who has believed our message and to whom has the arm of the Lord been revealed?"* (NIV). God has a written health plan filled with benefits for us, and the people who receive these medical benefits are those who put their trust in His report.

The Healing Creed is about the power of the redemptive blood of Jesus Christ to heal us in spirit, in soul, and in body. It is our foundation to believe for the miraculous. Read the healing creed aloud every day, and take note what starts to happen all around you.

THE HEALING CREED

I believe in Jesus Christ and in the power of His blood to heal (1 Pet. 2:24).

He bore my griefs, carried my sorrows and pains, was wounded for my transgressions, crushed for my wickedness, the punishment for my well-being fell upon Him, and by His wounds I am healed (Isa. 53:4-5).

I have been redeemed from the hand of the enemy (Ps. 107:2)—the thief, the devil who comes to steal, to kill, and to destroy (John 10:10)—and loosed from the contents within his hand, the curse (Gal. 3:13), and delivered from the spirit of fear and the power of death (Heb. 2:14-15; 2 Tim. 1:7).

I am an ambassador of Christ (2 Cor. 5:20); as Jesus is, so am I on this earth (1 John 4:17). Like Him, I humbly walk in the power of the fruits of the Spirit (Gal. 5:22-23)—love, joy, peace, longsuffering, kindness, goodness, faithfulness, gentleness, and self-control. So that I can effectively carry out official kingdom business, such as to heal and be healed for His glory.

I possess His authority over satan and all of his wicked works (Luke 10:19), including sickness and disease. Therefore, no weapon formed against me shall prosper (Isa. 54:17), nor will any plague come near my dwelling (Ps. 91:10).

I bless the sweet Lamb of God; I remember all of His benefits, who pardons all iniquities, heals all disease, redeems my life from destruction, crowns me with lovingkindness and tender mercies, satisfies my mouth with good things, and renews my youth like the eagle's (Ps. 103:1–5).

I am grateful that You are both able and willing (Luke 5:12-13) to heal me in spirit, soul, and body (1 Thess. 5:23). I partake of Your bread of life and drink from the cup of Your new covenant (John 6:35; 1 Cor. 11:23–32) to restore health to me and to heal me of my wounds (Prov. 4:20–22) with Your healing balm of Gilead (Jer. 30:17; 8:22).

Jehovah Rapha is my great physician (Exod. 15:26). His medical report declares (Isa. 53) His Spirit gives life to my mortal body (Rom. 8:11), and my faith makes me whole (Matt. 9:22).

I accept His advice to choose life that I may live (Deut. 30:19). I receive beauty for ashes, the oil of joy for mourning, the garment of praise for the spirit of heaviness (Isa. 61:3). I take His medicine— laughter (Prov. 17:22) and joy for my strength (Neh. 8:10).

I heed His counsel and repent (1 John 1:9), rid myself of bitterness (Prov. 17:22), forgive others (Matt. 6:14), and empower my faith by love (Gal. 5:6).

With wisdom from on high (James 3:17) I activate the Sword of the Spirit (Eph. 6:17). With the realization that I possess the power of life and death in my tongue (Prov. 18:21) I exercise His authority (Luke 10:19). And I curse this sickness at its very root and seed (Mark 11:12–24) and say no disease will prosper in my body (Isa. 54:17). When I am weak I thank Him that He remains strong in me (2 Cor. 12:9–11). And I boldly declare His abundant life, healing power, and supernatural strength to overtake my body (Rom. 4:17; Isa. 40:29,31) in Jesus' name (John 14:13-14; 15:16; 16:23-24,26).

I encourage you to read the healing creed aloud every day and allow its message to grab ahold of your spiritual heart and pump life into your physical being.

✝

CHAPTER 1

BELIEVE AGAIN

"I believe in Jesus Christ and in the
power of His blood to heal."

The other night, I saw in a dream a tall, barren tree planted by a brook that flowed with life in the midst of a bountiful meadow. Beneath the tree sat many of God's people, and all were bound to their wheelchairs. They leaned to the side because they lacked the strength to sit upright. They were pale and lifeless, but what disturbed me the most was the look of despair on their faces as they looked up toward Heaven convinced that God was not willing to heal them and even doubtful that He was able.

Psalm 1:3 clearly paints a picture of the blessed man or woman of God *"like a tree firmly planted by streams of water, which yields its fruit in its season and its leaf does not wither; and in whatever he does, he prospers"* (NASB). This is how we are to be—blessed because we live and have our being by the Living Water, nourished by His benefits, and producing fruit to give to others.

Yet the interpretation of the dream is revealing that the body of Christ is opposing God's health plan. Even though the planting of the tree is by streams of water and it should be flourishing, it is not. Instead it is rotting at the roots, decaying from the inside to the outside, and losing the beauty of God's benefits.

Why? What's wrong? On the whole, the Church is spiritually crippled and will not take the first step of faith. Many people who profess to be Christians, whether they are laypeople or in Church leadership, are more comfortable to walk in the counsel of the wicked, stand in the path of sinners, sit in the seat of scoffers, and blame God for their trouble. But instead of this they should meditate on the Word of God and do what it says to do, "Believe!" (See Psalm 1:1-2.)

As a prophetic healing evangelist, I have never seen so many of God's people as sick as they are today. This isn't right. The body of Christ needs to learn how to believe once again, exercise their authority as true believers, take a stand against the enemy and all of his wickedness, and overcome the situation that has them bound.

WHY DO GOD'S PEOPLE RESIST HIS HEALING POWER?

There are many reasons why God's people resist His healing power, but here are probably the most common reasons.

1. In general, the Church has kept silent about the healing power of Christ.

2. There is great confusion as to whether or not God wills to heal.

3. People have a negative image of God as being harsh and uncaring.

4. There's a fear of not being good enough to receive a blessing, such as healing from God.

5. The body of Christ has compromised and turns to everything else but the Lord for their healing.

Do You Welcome Jesus and His Healing Power?

Jesus is both willing and able to heal, but He gives us the responsibility of a free will. He respects the authority of the house. When the authority of the house surrenders to His ultimate authority, His healing power releases and heals. Let's look to the following example found in Luke 8:40–56 to understand what I mean.

Here we read the testimony of how a man named Jairus invites Jesus to his house to heal his sick daughter. Jesus agrees to go with him to his house but has another woman to attend to first. In the meantime, Jairus' daughter dies. When they arrive, Jesus encounters doubt and unbelief. He tries to encourage the people to believe, but they only laugh at Him. But because Jesus has the go-ahead from the authority of that household, Jairus and his wife, He ministers to their daughter.

Before He can do so, He has to kick the doubt and unbelief out. In other words, He makes the doubters leave the room and shuts the door and only allows those who believe with Him—Peter, James, and John and the girl's parents. He then raises her from the dead.

When we, the Church, align ourselves with God's healing message, the bondage of suffering is broken, and God's people are healed in spirit, in soul, and in body. This is when we witness the blind see, the deaf hear, the mute speak, the paralytics walk, cancers and every other deadly disease healed in Jesus' name.

I am grateful for our local pastor. He invites my husband and me to come in and teach the congregation everything we know about healing and miracles. He, along with the members, takes notes, puts his faith into action, participates with the people in healing outreaches, and encourages the congregation to minister healing to one another during Sunday morning services. And when there is a serious health issue, the people rally around that one with faith and see them healed. Because of it, our local fellowship witnesses healings and miracles. And you know what, the people are healthier.

Supernatural healing from the Lord causes the local body of Christ to strengthen in the power of faith, and even causes the ingathering to grow in great numbers, see the Book of Acts.

In another situation, the healing message was not welcomed, and Jesus could hardly do anything. Let's look at this portion of Scripture found in Mark 6:1–6. Here Jesus was in His hometown and was not able to heal more than a few people because the power of unbelief stopped Him from healing the people.

When unbelieving leaders—such as pastors, elders, board members, and the like—stop the move of the healing power of the Holy Spirit, it is deadly to the members of the congregations and just plain evil in the sight of our Lord.

Is it right that those who are in a battle for their life have to take a stand against the doubt and unbelief in the leadership in their local fellowship, quit, and seek out another fellowship where the people who claim to believe actually believe?

Do these people not have something more important to fight against? Yes, they do. They need to use every bit of faith they have and fight the main devil warring against them—death. They should not have to take on your little devils of doubt and unbelief. But, you see, your little devils of doubt and unbelief strengthen the bigger devil, death, that fights to take them down.

The same is true in the individual family unit. When I hear, for example, a woman speak from her deathbed that her husband will be angry with her if she fights to live again, something is seriously wrong.

We who declare that we believe in Jesus Christ must find our way back to the truth of His healing word so that those in our midst can receive their healing.

So with the responsibility of a free will, do we welcome or reject Jesus and His healing power?

RESTORE HOPE

It's time to look at another aspect of healing that we have to deal with in regard to God's healing power and the world's opinion of us for believing.

The world accuses us of being in denial if we do not accept their death sentence when attacked with sickness and disease. But what we have to understand when dealing with them is that even if their intentions are good they still do not possess the hope that we have in Christ. They are hopeless, literally people without hope, because they do not believe in the redemptive blood of Christ.

As Christians, we live in this world, but we are not to be of this world or worldly in our beliefs, words, or actions. We are to be people of faith, and faith begins with hope in our Savior and in what He has done for us.

Proverbs 13:12 tells us that, *"Hope deferred makes the heart sick, but when the desire comes, it is a tree of life."* So then why would we, as followers of Jesus Christ, steal a loved one's hope to believe for healing? Why would we discourage their faith to believe for their miracle from Jesus?

While in prayer with a couple of friends concerning this issue of unbelief within the body of Christ for healing, I saw in a vision Jesus walk toward a banquet table. He had on a light blue tunic with a multicolored sash and a prayer shawl covering His head, and He carried a shepherd's staff in His right hand. But the emphasis of the beginning of the vision was on His feet that were shod with leather sandals as our Shepherd walked upon dry, hard-packed ground toward a banquet table.

This first part of this vision reveals to us how He walks in His authority as the Good Shepherd and goes out to gather in His lost and hurting sheep to bring them back into the fold. He also reveals the spiritual condition of His people—they are spiritually dried up, and their hearts have been hardened to Him and His ways.

But He is a good shepherd, His love is unconditional, and with His staff He leads us and guides us into all truth by His righteousness. By wearing His prayer shawl He activates His love by the power of intercession for us.

The saints of God sat around this table with eating utensils in their hands pounding their fists upon the table. They were dissatisfied because there was no food or drink for them to partake of, and the head seat at the table was missing their Savior.

But Jesus did not disappoint those that turned to Him. I saw Him as He hung upon the Cross. His head dropped to His chest as He had suffered and died for them. He had paid the price with His own blood to put an end to their suffering.

He then raised His nail-pierced hands, and the blessings flowed through the holes in His hands. I then saw the people as they were plunged into the River of Life. They were fully immersed in the living water, and with their eating utensils still in their hands I could see them feasting upon the resurrection power of our Lord.

ENCOURAGE PEOPLE TO BELIEVE

As I mentioned earlier, it is wrong when leaders steal the hope of the people to believe God for their miracles. It's not right that God's people have to search outside of their local place of worship to find someone who will stand and believe with them for their healing. It is a disgrace to the Gospel of Jesus Christ when those who are in need of a miracle have to fight their fellow Christians for their spiritual right to believe for divine healing.

We ought to readily take upon ourselves the attribute of Barnabas, who was known in the Book of Acts as a believer in Jesus who gave encouragement to others. We should especially encourage the body of Christ to believe and stand with them to receive all that Jesus has for them instead of acting like a doubting Thomas and discouraging others from the faith with our words of doubt and unbelief.

Human reasoning does not please God; only faith does. It takes faith to initiate a move of God, and the precursor of faith according to Hebrews 11:1 is hope: *"Now faith is the substance of things hoped for, the evidence of things not seen."* The only way that people will be able to activate the power of faith for an unseen healing or miracle is that they first receive a message of hope to believe.

The underlying message of the Gospel is about hope in Jesus Christ. Hope to overcome against all odds.

OFFER HOPE FOR HEALING

Many people around us have received devastating reports of pain and death. They feel frightened and hopeless. We have a life-changing message to offer to them. A message of hope and healing for those that are sick and hurting.

But sometimes we feel insecure to deliver this message. What if they refuse the message? In all honesty, I have offered this message to thousands of people and have only ever had a few refuse prayer. What should this tell us? People want hope, and they are waiting for someone to offer to minister healing to them.

A REASON TO BELIEVE

In the news, whether the source is secular or Christian, you read or hear about how sickness, disease, plagues, pain, and suffering are on the rise. Have you ever wondered why these devilish things are increasing?

When we preach from human reasoning instead of the truth found in Scripture, people suffer. When we put all our faith in the doctor's report in place of the Bible, miracles cease. When we trust secular psychology rather than heed biblical counsel, healing is hindered.

We suffer from unanswered prayers when we give in to the world's system of doubt and unbelief, but we can change the situation around. In order to do so, we need a reason to believe. Let's look to the Word, find our reason to trust God, and believe again.

Six Reasons Why We Can Trust God to Keep His Promises

Even when people fail us, and they will, God can be trusted to keep all of His promises to us.

He is truthful.

God is not a man, that He should lie, nor a son of man, that He should repent. Has He said, and will He not do? Or has He spoken, and will He not make it good? (Numbers 23:19)

He is just.

He is the Rock, His work is perfect; for all His ways are justice, a God of truth and without injustice; righteous and upright is He (Deuteronomy 32:4).

He is able.

And being fully convinced that what He had promised He was also able to perform (Romans 4:21).

He is willing.

Then Jesus put out His hand and touched him, saying, "I am willing; be cleansed." Immediately his leprosy was cleansed (Matthew 8:3).

He is faithful.

He who calls you is faithful, who also will do it (1 Thessalonians 5:24).

His faithfulness is unconditional.

If we are faithless, He remains faithful; He cannot deny Himself (2 Timothy 2:13).

If we will spend time and meditate upon these Scriptures we will find our reason to trust in God to keep His promises.

How Do We Develop Faith to Believe?

Our faith to believe for healing will develop as we learn to trust in God's faithfulness to keep His promise to heal. The Scriptures tell us in

Romans 10:17, *"So then faith comes by hearing, and hearing by the word of God."* As we spend time in God's Word concerning healing, the Holy Spirit reveals to us the truth, and what was once a challenge now becomes easy to believe. First Corinthians 2:14 puts it like this, *"But the natural man does not receive the things of the Spirit of God, for they are foolishness to him; nor can he know them, because they are spiritually discerned."* Your faith to believe for healing will develop as you dig into God's Word about it.

A word of caution when developing your faith to believe for healing. Our enemy is a mastermind at distracting us, and not all of his schemes appear wicked. When you make the quality decision to zero in on healing, stay focused and be aware of his tactics of confusion and distractions that he will use to try to lure you away as you search out God's healing message. He doesn't want you to find your healing, but God does. So move forward and develop your faith to believe in healing.

BREAK THE CYCLE OF UNBELIEF

Some of you are still skeptical, but, you know, every person with a healing testimony in this book can come up with plenty of excuses not to believe God for their healings. The reality of the matter remains—they all have human wills and the freedom to choose. This is a powerful gift from Elohim, and if we will wield our will, bring it under submission to the Word of God, there's no telling what can happen.

But you see, we get brazened, hard-hearted towards God's goodness and His promise to heal so that we don't even think to trust God to heal us. We automatically turn to the world's methods first, and become discouraged, even to the point of hopelessness when our human efforts do not produce the desired results, health, healing, and wholeness.

But we can choose to break this cycle of unbelief in our life today. It starts with a quality decision to learn how to believe.

And while Jesus is bidding to all, *"If you can believe, all things are possible to him who believes."* A few of you are responding and calling out to

Him, even with tears, like the man in Mark 9:23-25, *"Lord, I believe; help my unbelief!"*

And our beautiful Savior, through His Word, honors this request and teaches us how to transform unbelief to belief.

Ten Steps to Learn to Believe Again

1. Acknowledge the sin of unbelief and repent from it. First John 1:9 says, *"If we confess our sins, He is faithful and just to forgive us our sins and to cleanse us from all unrighteousness."*

2. Ask the Holy Spirit to teach you how to heal. James 1:5 encourages us to ask, *"If any of you lacks wisdom, let him ask of God, who gives to all liberally and without reproach, and it will be given to him."*

3. Read and study the Word concerning healing. Second Timothy 2:15 admonishes us to, *"Do your best to present yourself to God as one approved, a worker who does not need to be ashamed and who correctly handles the word of truth"* (NIV).

4. Mediate upon the healing Scriptures morning, noon, and night. Joshua 1:8 gives us the results: *"This Book of the Law shall not depart from your mouth, but you shall meditate in it day and night, that you may observe to do according to all that is written in it. For then you will make your way prosperous, and then you will have good success."*

5. With the blessing of technology, listen to healing sermons over and over again. Romans 10:17 tells us how faith comes: *"So then faith comes by hearing, and hearing by the word of God."*

6. Take every negative thought captive that rises up against healing. Second Corinthians 10:4-5 teaches us about spiritual warfare concerning our thoughts, *"For the weapons*

of our warfare are not carnal but mighty in God for pulling down strongholds, casting down arguments and every high thing that exalts itself against the knowledge of God, bringing every thought into captivity to the obedience of Christ."

7. Refrain from depressing media about people dying from sickness and disease, such as faithless movies and reading materials. Proverbs 4:23 gives warning: *"Above all else, guard your heart, for everything you do flows from it"* *(NIV).*

8. Choose your friends wisely; if they discourage your faith to believe, pray for someone who will believe with you. First Corinthians 15:33 states the importance of choosing friends wisely. It says, *"Do not be deceived: 'Evil company corrupts good habits.'"*

9. Make sure that your words declare God's healing power. Proverbs 18:21 teaches us about the power of the tongue. It declares, *"Death and life are in the power of the tongue, and those who love it will eat its fruit."*

10. Your actions must line up with healing as well. James 2:17 tells us that, *"In the same way, faith by itself, if it is not accompanied by action, is dead"* (NIV).

These ten steps will radically change your life. Your faith to believe for supernatural healing from Jesus will be empowered, supercharged, and will produce health and healing. We will delve deeper into each of these steps throughout this work.

WHAT DOES GOD SAY ABOUT HIMSELF AND HEALING?

The next time someone tries to steal your hope for healing, don't listen. Instead, read God's Word and find out what He has to say about the matter. Here are a couple scriptures to help you get started on your healing journey.

I, the Lord, am your healer (Exodus 15:26 NASB).

"For I will restore health to you and heal you of your wounds," *says the Lord* (Jeremiah 30:17).

HOPE AND FAITH EMPLOY SUPERNATURAL HEALING

Elizabeth from Harrisonburg, Virginia received a series of remarkable miracles in one night when her hope and faith employed supernatural healing. Let's read her amazing story.

While at work at the local meat factory, she drops a large piece of frozen meat and breaks the bones in both of her feet. She walks slowly and with tremendous pain. Later, she hears of a healing service and decides to come. Her faith activates to believe for her feet to be healed. She receives a healing touch, and the next morning she runs up and down the stairs with no pain and she even stands on her tiptoes.

Not only is her faith inspired to receive healing for her feet that night, but it is emboldened to believe to be healed from thyroid disease.

The same healing hands that release the power of the Holy Spirit to heal her broken feet also release healing from thyroid disease. Again, that next morning amazing manifestations are exhibiting themselves. While asleep during the night she loses four pounds, and the growth on the side of her neck disappears.

Because her hope transforms into faith for miraculous healing, her testimony increases in its brilliance. Before she attends this healing service, she is also a victim of heart disease. Her doctor tells her that she is going to have a heart attack. In other words, before this spiritual transformation she lives with a nagging fear that she will have a heart attack. This is not a pleasant thought to live with.

But she receives an injection of hope to believe for healing from heart disease as well, and her faith activates and accesses the power of the Holy Spirit and she receives a new heart. Once again in this glorious morning, she realizes as she runs up the steps that she is not even out of breath. Before, these steps are laborsome for her, but not anymore!

Astonishing displays of the healing power of Jesus Christ will materialize when we release hope and faith to others to believe again.

Elizabeth has these words of encouragement for you, "The only thing I can say is that I am only human, that the Lord will do the same thing for anybody else that He will do for me. And I praise Him every day for the healing that I have received."

> *Dear Jesus,*
>
> *I do believe in You and in the power of Your blood to heal. I cry out to You to teach me how to transform my unbelief to belief in regard to my healing. I ask You, Holy Spirit, to uncover hidden doubts and expose the lies of the enemy that I accept as truth. Help me to break this cycle of unbelief that binds me to sickness and disease. Teach me how to think, speak, and act according to Your healing word.*
>
> *In Your name, Jesus, I pray, amen.*

The foundation of our faith to believe for healing is the redemptive blood of Jesus Christ. Turn to the next chapter to find out what Jesus does for us so we can activate His healing message.

✝

SELF-EXAMINATION

Do I need healing? Do I have the faith to believe for my healing? Is the message of healing new to me? Or have I walked away from this message? If so, do I know why I lost hope in His healing power? More importantly, do I know how to believe again for my healing?

✝

Chapter 2

THE POWER OF THE BLOOD

"He bore my griefs, carried my sorrows and pains,
was wounded for my transgressions, crushed for my
wickedness, the punishment for my well-being fell
upon Him, and by His wounds I am healed."

There was a time not so long ago that the Church readily taught and sang about the redemptive blood of Jesus Christ. On a whole, the body of Christ walked in authority over satan and his wicked works. As a result she was stronger and healthier. Nowadays, it is rare to hear a pastor teach this message, and because of the lack of this teaching, God's people are sick and weak. But I want to encourage you to release this life-changing message from your pulpit once again.

I believe in the healing power of the redemptive blood of Jesus Christ—so much so that I teach it everywhere I go. Because I do, I consistently witness the power of the Spirit move in stunning and supernatural ways—the blind see, the deaf hear, the paralytics walk, sick people are healed, and demons flee by the power of the blood.

The blood of Jesus is not dried up. It's fresh, alive, and all-powerful. When we accept this revelation, we can activate His authority and release the captives from the bondage of satan, including ourselves.

Recently during one particular healing service, I used an interpreter to translate the message into the language of the local people. I was midway into the lesson when all of a sudden the interpreter started to shout. "I can't do this! This is too hard for me! Will someone please pray for me?"

I reached my hand out and touched him on the shoulder and prayed for him. Then all of a sudden, the young man ran out of the sanctuary and into the hallway. It caused a great disruption in the meeting, and the people stood up to watch him. I was able to get the people to sit down, and we continued on with the meeting. But what I was not able to see from the pulpit was the young man as he began to vomit.

What happened during this healing service? Unbeknownst to me, this nice young man was not born again, and the demon within him could not handle the message of the redemptive blood of Jesus Christ. It cried out, "I can't do this! This is too hard for me!"

In front of everyone was a display of spiritual warfare, and the power in the blood to set the captive free. The spirit of the young man cried out, "Will someone please pray for me?" I reached my hand out to touch the young man and began to pray. It was more than the demon could handle. The only chance it had to remain in control of the young man was to cause him to run away from the power of the blood, but it was too late—too much revelation concerning the blood of Christ had been revealed. The young man was delivered and vomited the evil spirit out.

At the end of this service, when the altar call was given he was the first to come forward, kneel, and receive Christ as his Savior.

I have seen time and time again as I preach about the blood, that supernatural power is released and the demons residing within the unregenerated souls are literally tormented and they scream and act out in terror. And the people are delivered, set free, born again, and healed in spirit, in soul, and in body.

I can't encourage you enough to get back to the message of the blood. Study the Scriptures and activate this power in your personal life and in your ministry today.

By His Stripes We Are Healed

Surely He has borne our griefs and carried our sorrows; yet we esteemed Him stricken, smitten by God, and afflicted. But He was wounded for our transgressions, He was bruised for our iniquities; the chastisement for our peace was upon Him, and by His stripes we are healed (Isaiah 53:4-5).

Time and time again, I witness the manifest power of the blood in this portion of Scripture. I can tell you firsthand, this message literally torments satan and his demons. It's here where they encounter their defeat, and they fear when we hear its truth.

They witnessed this event through their own eyes of deception. Later when Jesus rose from the dead, the truth was revealed, and they knew they were defeated for eternity because of this historical event recorded in Isaiah 53:4-5.

This is why demonic forces fight so hard to create controversy with this foundational truth. They realize that if they spread false teaching amongst the body of Christ concerning supernatural healing, people will be weak in the faith, powerless against their wicked attacks, bound by sickness and disease, tormented in their minds and emotions, and live in defeat. This will cause them to be ineffective with their witness to the lost.

The "By His Stripes" Controversy

There is great controversy amongst the Church today as to whether or not the scriptural meaning of Isaiah 53:5, *"by His stripes we are healed,"* refers to spiritual, emotional, or physical healing.

Obviously, the prophet Isaiah knew that God's people would doubt physical healing, because Isaiah 53 starts out with him questioning the reader, *"Who has believed our report?"* (Isa. 53:1). The Holy Spirit gave him an in-depth supernatural understanding of how the Messiah would embrace great suffering for our redemption so that we could be healed. He also gave him the revelation knowledge that there would be great debate, even division, about the power of the atoning blood of Christ that was shed as they whipped His back to include physical healing.

Some firmly believe this refers to spiritual healing only, meaning that the sole purpose of the atonement is to forgive us of our sins so that we can be reconciled back to our heavenly Father and have eternal life with Him through the sufferings of Christ. And yes, Jesus did suffer for this purpose, and we are not to take our eternal salvation lightly. But this is not the only reason for the atonement. It is the beginning of the redemption process.

Others believe that this healing is spiritual, as discussed above, and emotional or mental, meaning healing of past hurts and disappointments, but certainly not physical healing.

Now that we all understand what the "by His stripes" controversy is, let's work to resolve the chaos.

END THE CONTROVERSY NOW

In order to end this controversy within our own hearts, let's do a word search with the online Blue Letter Bible[1] and find out what this portion of Scripture really means.

Let's start with "He has borne our griefs." According to *Strong's Concordance* number H2483, *griefs* or the Hebrew word *choliy* means sickness.

Then let's go to "and carried our sorrows." The Strong's definition for H4341, the word *sorrows* or the Hebrew word *mak'ob,* means both mental and physical pain.

As we continue on it says that "He was bruised for our iniquities." According to Strong's definition H5771, the word *iniquities* translated from the Hebrew word *'avon* and means perversity or sin.

Now, we will check out the word *healed* from the portion of Scripture that says *"by His stripes we are healed."* The Strong's reference number

H7495 for this word comes from the Hebrew word *rapha'*, which means healer, to cure, heal, repair, and make whole.

When we spend the time and rightly divide the Word, we can determine that the translation of Isaiah 53:4-5 is holistic. That the atonement, the redemptive blood of Jesus, does in fact provide spiritual, emotional, and physical healing.

I've included a chart of Hebrew words and their meanings found in Isaiah 53:4-5 to help you have a clearer understanding of what Jesus endured for us.

Hebrew Words and Their Meanings in Isaiah 53:4-5

PORTION OF SCRIPTURE	ENGLISH	HEBREW	DEFINITION	STRONG'S REFERENCE
He bore our griefs	Bore	nasa'	to bear, carry	H5375
	Griefs	choliy	sickness	H2483
He carried our sorrows	Carried	cabal	to bear	H5445
	Sorrows	mak'ob	physical and mental pain	H4341
Yet, we esteemed Him stricken, smitten by God	Esteem	chashab	to make a judgement	H2803
	Stricken	naga'	plague	H5060
	Smitten	nakah	slaughter	H5221
He was wounded for our transgressions	Wounded	chalal	defile	H2490
	Transgression	pesha'	rebellion	H6588
He was bruised for our iniquities	Bruised	daka'	to crush	H1792
	Iniquities	'avon	perversity, sin	H5771

PORTION OF SCRIPTURE	ENGLISH	HEBREW	DEFINITION	STRONG'S REFERENCE
The chastisement for our peace was upon Him	Chastisement	muwcar	discipline, correction	H4148
	Peace	shalowmn	welfare, i.e. health, prosperity, peace	H7965
By His stripes we are healed	Stripes	chabbuwrah	bruise, stripe, wound	H2250
	Healed	rapha'	cure, heal, make whole	H7495

In conclusion to this word study of Isaiah 53:4-5, we discover that Jesus bore or carried our sickness and our physical and mental pain upon His own body for us. Even though innocent, He was plagued and slaughtered as our judgement fell upon Him. He was defiled for our rebellion. He was crushed for our perversity and sin. He took upon Himself our discipline and correction for our welfare, health, prosperity, and peace. He was bruised, striped or whipped and wounded, so we could be cured, healed, and made whole.

INTENSE WHIPPING

The whippings that Jesus received because of us and for us were intense. Let's focus on the intensity to gain understanding of what He had to endure for our healing.

Psalm 22 is a graphic prophecy about the anguish that Jesus would suffer for us. Let's read verses 14–19 together and open up our spiritual ears and listen to the cry of His heart to the Father.

I am poured out like water, and all My bones are out of joint;
My heart is like wax; it has melted within Me. My strength

is dried up like a potsherd, and My tongue clings to My jaws; You have brought Me to the dust of death. For dogs have surrounded Me; the congregation of the wicked has enclosed Me. They pierced My hands and My feet; I can count all My bones. They look and stare at Me. They divide My garments among them, and for My clothing they cast lots. But You, O Lord, do not be far from Me; O My Strength, hasten to help Me!

Jesus had been betrayed, falsely accused, arrested, and interrogated during the night at an illegal, secret trial. He suffered from great emotional anguish to the point of bleeding and was also sleep deprived.

He was abandoned, criticized, cursed at, devalued, humiliated, mocked, ridiculed, spit upon, and stripped physically and emotionally. He had no strength left; He was literally spent.

He was in excruciating pain because they beat upon Him, ripped His beard off His face, pierced His skull with a crown of thorns, whipped Him mercilessly, nailed His hands and feet to the Cross, and his bones were dislocated from the weight of the crossbeam that He had to carry and from the position He was strung up on the Cross. His heart was overworked, stressed out, and at the point of death.

In regard to the severity of being whipped for our healing it says in verse 17, *"I can count all My bones."* What horrible suffering! The bones in His body were exposed. He could see and count them. In order for Him to be able to count His bones, that means His skin, muscles, ligaments, tendons, and nerves had to be ripped apart. His blood was spilled as they whipped Him to pieces for payment for our emotional and physical healing.

ACTIVATE THE POWER OF THE BLOOD

On another occasion, during the message of the blood at a healing service a man was thrown down on the floor by an epileptic spirit and started to convulse. As I began to quote this Scripture, the demon in this man became extremely violent and began to thrash and scream and eventually began to beg for me to stop. I would not.

I continued on with the message of the blood for this man's deliverance. When I spoke about how Jesus was whipped for this man's physical healing, the demon went completely mad and was tortured by the power of the blood. It actually began to spit blood in my face and begged me to stop.

This demon had a lifelong hold on this man's life and didn't want to leave, but by the time I finished declaring the message of the blood the demon released him, and the man was healed spiritually, emotionally, and physically.

Breakdown of His Healing

Spiritual Healing

* Deliverance from demon possession.

* Repentance of past sins.

* Accepted Christ as his Savior.

* Received the baptism of the Holy Spirit.

Emotional or Mental Healing

* Through deliverance his mind and emotions were healed from fear and depression.

Physical Healing

* He was physically healed from epilepsy.

Can you imagine what would happen if the Church repented and returned back to the message of the blood? How many people would turn to Christ and have their needs met?

Let's pray this prayer of repentance together and start fresh again.

Dear Jesus,

As we take the time to contemplate what You actually did for us, our hearts are filled with sorrow for the pain that we caused You. We are forever grateful that You bore all of our sickness, all of our physical and emotional pain upon Your own body for us.

It grieves our spirits to realize that even though You were innocent, You were plagued and slaughtered as our judgement fell upon You. If we could only go back and undo the past...but we know we can't. So we face up and acknowledge our guilt, and we are truly sorry that because of our wrongdoing You were defiled for our rebellion and crushed for our perversity and willful sin. Please, forgive us.

Out of Your love for us, You were disciplined and corrected for our welfare, health, prosperity, and peace. You were bruised, striped, whipped, and wounded so that we could be cured, healed, and made whole. We thank You, Jesus, for this.

Hear our cry of repentance for doubting Your healing power to heal us spiritually, emotionally, and physically. Forgive us for placing such a low value on Your blood and upon Your sufferings for us. Again, we thank You for the full payment for our health and well-being. And we ask You, please help us to start to heal again.

In Your name we pray, dear Jesus, amen.

Read the next chapter to find out what our Redeemer saved us from.

✝

SELF-EXAMINATION

Do I understand what the blood of Jesus Christ did for me? Have I personally experienced the power of His blood to heal me in my emotions and in my physical body? If not, am I willing to receive His healing power in me?

NOTE

1. Hebrew word definitions are provided by *Strong's Concordance* and can be found at *Blue Letter Bible*: https://www.blueletterbible .org.

CHAPTER 3

MY REDEEMER

"I have been redeemed from the hand of the enemy, the thief, the devil who comes to steal, to kill, and to destroy, and loosed from the contents within his hand, the curse, and delivered from the spirit of fear and the power of death."

I grew up in a denominational church. I was baptized as an infant, attended Sunday school and Sunday morning services with my family, was confirmed in my teenage years, and yet I had no understanding of what Jesus Christ really did for me. I did not understand that church attendance wasn't enough but that I needed to be born again. I certainly did not receive teaching about the redemptive blood of Jesus Christ to heal the sick.

I'm almost embarrassed, but nevertheless I will share this with you to help you be free from a damaging perception many have about our Lord. I remember when I was a young Christian mama and I was expecting our third child. I went into premature labor and was put on bedrest for six weeks. I have a vivid memory of myself on my knees in the living room crying and begging God not to take the life of my baby. I was even bargaining with Him and told Him that if He would spare the life of my child I would not have another. As if God was my enemy who was attempting to steal my baby away from me because He was angry with me for expecting another child and that coming to Jesus with a need for my unborn child was a bother to Him.

Do you hear the negative mindset that I had toward God? I was a new believer, only a few years old in the Lord, and my mind was in need of renewal to cleanse it from negative, religious beliefs about our God. Beliefs that I did not realize I even had.

As I look back at this incident in my life, I can quickly discern that I thought of God as having an evil streak in Him. I did not know how to rightly judge what was happening to me. Obviously, I was downright confused, and I was blaming Jesus for the wicked works of satan.

I was unenlightened about the true character and nature of God in this area, and healing was foreign to me. I had to learn that God was not my enemy but my friend, my helper, my redeemer, and He wanted to give life and not take it from me.

I believe the main reason Christian people are sick and dying prematurely today is that the Church on a whole has taken the healing message and shoved it in a closet and locked the door behind them. It is time to unlock the door and allow people to hear the Good News about a loving God who cares so much for us that He provides us with the gifts of supernatural healing so we can have a foundation of faith to stand upon to believe and receive healing when we have needs.

If God's Word teaches us that we can build our faith to believe for the miraculous by listening to His healing Word, then I suggest we do just that—dust off our Bibles, read and study the healing Scriptures, meditate upon His healing message, and do what He tells us to do.

Let's begin educating ourselves about supernatural healing by first examining the words *save* and *saved*. There are other biblical definitions for these common words that are important for us to understand, that will cause our faith to arise and believe God not only for eternal life but for the miraculous on this earth as well.

Let's review the following scriptures to discover the meaning of these all-important and eternal words for us.

And she shall bring forth a son, and thou shalt call his name Jesus: for he shall save his people from their sins (Matthew 1:21 KJV).

If you confess with your mouth the Lord Jesus and believe in your heart that God has raised Him from the dead, you will be saved (Romans 10:9).

For God did not send His Son into the world to condemn the world, but that the world through Him might be saved (John 3:17).

In each of these well-known verses, the words *save* or *saved* are derived from the same Greek word, *sōzō,* and have the same meaning—*to save, deliver, protect, heal, preserve, do well, and be made whole* (Strong's, G4982). This proves to us that our salvation in Christ Jesus goes beyond eternal life in Heaven and includes divine health and healing for us while on this earth.

Many Christians have bought into the lie that we will be healed when we are in Heaven. This may sound logical to some, but it is not biblical. Sickness and disease do not exist in Heaven. They cannot enter into Heaven's gates. Heaven is not in a fallen state, but earth is. Therefore, on this earth is where we need His healing power to manifest, not in Heaven.

According to Acts 4:12, there is only one name that we can be saved by, and that name is Jesus Christ. And First Corinthians 1:30 describes what our Redeemer is for us: *"But of Him you are in Christ Jesus, who became for us wisdom from God—and righteousness and sanctification and redemption."*

HE IS OUR WISDOM

But the wisdom that is from above is first pure, then peaceable, gentle, willing to yield, full of mercy and good fruits, without partiality and without hypocrisy (James 3:17).

Wisdom takes knowledge, facts, and information and puts them into practice. As the redeemed in Christ, we are to take hold of His knowledge and His ways and live them. In regard to His healing message, we are to take possession of His healing promise and allow it to manifest in our human bodies.

Like Elizabeth, who we read about in Chapter 1, when she heard the biblical evidence for supernatural healing, even though it went against all human reasoning and the five senses, she could not deny the wisdom from above that imparted God's peace, gentleness, and His mercy toward her without partiality. She knew that she knew healing belonged to her, and because she received God's wisdom concerning healing, she was healed from broken bones in her feet, thyroid disease, and heart disease too.

HE IS OUR RIGHTEOUSNESS

For He made Him who knew no sin to be sin for us, that we might become the righteousness of God in Him (2 Corinthians 5:21).

We cannot become the righteousness of God by our good works—only by the redemptive work of our Redeemer. As our Redeemer, He paid the price with His blood so that we can activate His *sōzō* power in our lives and, yes, be delivered from eternal damnation, but also that we could be healed in spirit, in soul, and in body.

Oftentimes, people struggle with supernatural healing because of their past. Whether they were the culprit or the victim, they do not believe that they are good enough to receive God's blessings, including healing. Yes, if we were to stand upon our own righteousness we would never be good enough to receive His gifts. Thankfully it is not our good deeds that we stand upon to receive healing, but upon the righteousness of Jesus Christ.

Isaiah 53:4-5 paints a clear picture of what Jesus suffered so that we can take upon His righteousness. His blood covers all sin that we have committed or has been done against us. We do need to activate the power of His blood by asking Him to forgive us or to forgive those who have wronged us. Then we are clean and free from guilt and shame.

> *If we [freely] admit that we have sinned and confess our sins, He is faithful and just [true to His own nature and promises], and will forgive our sins and cleanse us continually from all unrighteousness [our wrongdoing, everything not in conformity with His will and purpose]* (1 John 1:9 AMP).

Because of what Jesus suffered for us, we can freely put on the breastplate of His righteousness (see Eph. 6:14), and rely on His good works and not upon ours to believe and receive His healing touch.

HE IS OUR SANCTIFICATION

> *Do you not know that the unrighteous will not inherit the kingdom of God? Do not be deceived. Neither fornicators, nor idolaters, nor adulterers, nor homosexuals, nor sodomites, nor thieves, nor covetous, nor drunkards, nor revilers, nor extortioners will inherit the kingdom of God. And such were some of you. But you were washed, but you were sanctified, but you were justified in the name of the Lord Jesus and by the Spirit of our God* (1 Corinthians 6:9–11).

Sin prevents us from receiving our God-given inheritance, and living a life of sin stops us from entering into His kingdom. But again, our Redeemer has come to our rescue and sanctifies us, washes us, and makes us clean. Our Redeemer spiritually cleanses those of us who will believe in Him. This is the reason we can come to Him as we are and receive all of His benefits, including emotional and physical healing.

Recently, I ministered to a young man in a healing service who struggled to be free in Christ for things that took place in his past. The Holy Spirit revealed the hurtful issues that brought him to the situation he is living in today.

As a young boy he was abandoned by both of his parents. This rejection left deep wounds and scars that led him down a dark path of satanic worship, substance abuse, and addictions. He was feeling so hopeless that he contemplated suicide that morning, but instead found himself weeping and crying out to his heavenly Father at the altar that morning for deliverance.

This young man is washed, sanctified, and justified not by His own strength but in the name of our Lord Jesus, who suffered and shed His blood for Him, and by the Spirit of God.

HE IS OUR REDEMPTION

In Him we have redemption through His blood, the forgiveness of sins, according to the riches of His grace (Ephesians 1:7).

By the riches of our Redeemer's grace, He has given to us an eternal inheritance that is above and beyond anything we can possibly imagine. If we would only tap into the supernatural *sōzō* power of His grace and receive all that He desires for us on this earth and in Heaven.

The word *redemption* means a releasing or liberation effected or procured by payment of ransom. For us, the blood of Christ was the payment necessary for our salvation, deliverance, and redemption.

Just like I began to discover God's goodness, you too can learn to believe that God is not the author of evil, but good. When you cleanse your heart from evil thoughts about Him, you will begin to trust Him as a friend and beyond. He's the friend who sticks closer than a brother in every situation you will face. You can witness the goodness of God in your life if you will start to trust in Him as your redeemer.

WHAT HAVE WE BEEN REDEEMED FROM?

According to Psalm 107:2, *"Let the redeemed of the Lord say so, whom He has redeemed from the hand of the enemy,"* and Galatians 3:13 tells us what is in his hand, *"Christ has redeemed us from the curse of the law, having become a curse for us (for it is written, 'Cursed is everyone who hangs on a tree').*" In other words, we have been redeemed from the hand of our enemy, satan. We have been liberated from what is within his hand, the curse. This curse is brought upon us by the old law, by our own willful disobedience to God, and through generational curses passed to us from our ancestors' past unconfessed sins against God.

What Is the Curse?

Simply put, the curse is anything activated against us that steals, kills, or destroys us in any area of life.

God gives us a list of what He considers to be the curse in Deuteronomy 28:15–68. This list includes such things as lack and poverty, drought and other harmful weather, vulnerability to our enemies and their terroristic attacks, barren wombs, boils, tumors, scabs, itches, diseased knees and legs that cannot be healed, madness, blindness, bewilderment of the heart, marital problems, livestock stolen and slaughtered, children taken away from their parents, the produce of your land lost to foreigners, and sickness and incurable disease. Basically, no matter where we are or what we do, the curse will follow us if we do not repent.

Who Is Responsible for the Curse?

One would think that the answer to this question is obvious, but to many of God's people it is not. Jesus tells us in John 10:10 that the thief, satan, comes to steal, to kill, and to destroy. He is the one who responsible for all of the evil rising against us. Satan is the author of doubt and unbelief, and he is our enemy. So let's do the right thing and get him out of our lives and live free from his heavy baggage that is weighing us down.

Jesus also makes it clear that He is different. He comes to give us life and to give it to us in abundance.

I use this verse to judge life's circumstances with. I ask myself, "Is someone or something trying to steal from me?" "Is this situation trying to kill me or produce death in any area of my life?" "Is this trying to wreak havoc or destruction in my life?" If the answer is yes to any of these three questions, I immediately know that this is an attack and that satan is behind it.

Likewise, if the situation is seeding something good, producing life, bringing about increase, and releasing godly benefits then I know that it is of God.

How Did Jesus Set Out to Undo the Curse?

First, He did the unthinkable—He humbled Himself. He left the glory of Heaven and came down to this earth in the most vulnerable form, a baby, and was born to an innocent young virgin named Mary in a stable because the world had no room for God's greatest gift—salvation.

Destined was He to be the sacrificial Lamb of God who would be slaughtered to release us from the bondage of satan and to liberate us from the curse of all his wicked works. Our Redeemer of His own accord would shed His own blood for the full payment for our redemption, including forgiveness of sins, deliverance from demonic oppression and possession, healing in the spirit, in soul, and in body, and all of His other benefits.

Part of this plan of redemption includes living a life that is not of this world but of God's kingdom. Demonstrating to us that a life based on faith in the promises of our God, release us from the constraints of this fallen world and into the fulfillment of His supernatural promises. Showing us that it is possible to live in victory by faith.

DELIVERED FROM A SPIRIT OF FEAR AND THE POWER OF DEATH

If the Lord should tarry, we will all die one day; this is the natural cycle of life that God has established. According to Ecclesiastes 3:2, there is a time to be born and a time to die. When we understand the character of God, we can accept godly death with a spirit of peace, especially when those who pass or are about to pass from this earth are in the Lord. We are to comfort one another with the following words:

But I do not want you to be ignorant, brethren, concerning those who have fallen asleep, lest you sorrow as others who have no hope. For if we believe that Jesus died and rose again, even so God will bring with Him those who sleep in Jesus. For this we say to you by the word of the Lord, that we who are alive and remain until the coming of the Lord will by no means precede those who are asleep. For the Lord Himself will descend from heaven with a shout, with the voice of an archangel, and with the trumpet of God. And the dead in Christ will rise first. Then we who are alive and remain shall be caught up together with them in the clouds to meet the Lord in the air. And thus we shall always be with the Lord. Therefore comfort one another with these words (1 Thessalonians 4:13–18).

God gave us His nature to protect ourselves and our loved ones from pain, suffering, and premature death. This is good, godly, and right. But many of God's people have an unnatural fear of death. Usually, this is because they are unlearned in the ways of the Lord concerning death, but are full of the world's thoughts about this matter. They fill themselves with negative and fear-filled reports from the world instead of focusing on the Word of God.

You know as well as I do that all we have to do is open up the newspaper or a magazine, turn on the television, or get on the Internet and we will be bombarded with negative reports of sickness, disease, and death. If we indulge in these negative messages, we will infect ourselves with seeds of doubt and unbelief in God's healing power and can become subject to a wicked spirit called "fear." The spirit of fear does not come from God and is a precursor to premature death.

The Bible warns us in Job 3:25, *"For the thing I greatly feared has come upon me, and what I dreaded has happened to me."*

If you receive a death report from your physician and desire to be healed supernaturally and live, you must bind up the spirit of fear and put it under your feet. In other words, you must activate your authority over this spirit of fear and over premature death. Otherwise, you will die prematurely from the supernatural power of the deathly attack rising against you.

According to Hebrews, Jesus has delivered you from the bondage of the fear of death. It says:

> *Inasmuch then as the children have partaken of flesh and blood, He Himself likewise shared in the same, that through death He might destroy him who had the power of death, that is, the devil, and release those who through fear of death were all their lifetime subject to bondage* (Hebrews 2:14-15).

FREEDOM FROM THE SPIRIT OF FEAR

Second Timothy 1:7 makes it clear what God has and has not given to us. It says, *"For God has not given us a spirit of fear, but of power and of love and of a sound mind."*

We need to get a handle on fear and cast it out of our lives once and for all. According to the Word, fear is an actual spirit, and God didn't give it to us. He wants us to be free from its terroristic attacks against us.

As mentioned earlier, the things we fear the most will come upon us. Ask yourself, "What am I afraid of?" And receive a word of advice, "Get rid of this evil spirit of fear!" Otherwise, this spirit will take control of you, and the thing you fear will manifest in your life.

Insurance versus Assurance

Let's look at another area where fear has people bound—insurance versus assurance. What happens when the insurance company informs you that it will no longer provide coverage for your present situation or pay for a certain medication or treatment that you have been told you need? Honestly, most of God's people will start to panic.

I'm telling you, God's people will hunt high and low and even travel to foreign countries to find these medications. Why? Because they are controlled by a spirit of fear that shouts to them that they are now going to die. They lack the assurance that Jesus is able and willing to heal them.

Where Can We Find This Assurance for Healing?

The assurance for divine healing comes from reading and studying God's contract, the Holy Bible, and then activating it by your signature of faith. When sickness and disease come upon you, you claim the benefits in this assurance policy.

DELIVERED FROM PARKINSON'S DISEASE

Betty from Harrisonburg, Virginia received revelation knowledge that set her free from the bondage of fear and the power of death via Parkinson's disease. What is the revelation that set her free?

Betty and her husband were taking turns reading from my last book, *Greater Than Magic,* when all of a sudden her husband called out to her and said, "Sweetheart, listen to this. 'Physical attacks are mere manifestations of spiritual ones.'"[1]

She answered, "What?" She immediately knew the interpretation to a dream she had a few days earlier.

In the dream she saw a woman with blond hair lying on her right side; her mouth was bound with gray duct tape, and her hands and feet were bound behind her back. Actually, this dream was so disturbing to her that she refrained from sharing it with her husband until this moment.

When he heard the dream he said, "You're telling me just now about this dream?" He continued, "The woman in the dream is you."

Betty realized what satan was trying to do to her. He was attacking her with Parkinson's disease. With this disease she was losing her voice and the strength in her hands and feet, and she wasn't very functional anymore. The enemy was trying to shut her down so that she could no longer talk, move, function, or do things on her own.

God told her that He would heal her as she goes. Just like He told the ten lepers:

Now it happened as He went to Jerusalem that He passed through the midst of Samaria and Galilee. Then as He entered a certain village, there met Him ten men who were lepers, who stood afar off. And they lifted up their voices and said, "Jesus, Master, have mercy on us!" So when He saw them, He said to them, "Go, show yourselves to the priests." And so it was that as they went, they were cleansed. And one of them, when he saw that he was healed, returned, and with a loud voice glorified God, and fell down on his face at His feet, giving Him thanks. And he was a Samaritan. So Jesus answered and said, "Were there not ten cleansed? But where are the nine? Were there not any found who returned to give glory to God except this foreigner?" And He said to him, "Arise, go your way. Your faith has made you well (Luke 17:11-19).

By the intervention of her Redeemer, the Lord Jesus Christ, Betty is redeemed, set free, and she no longer has Parkinson's disease.

We will read a little more in Chapter 7 about what happens to Betty as she shares her testimony at a recent healing seminar in her hometown.

PRAYER

Dear Jesus,

You are my redeemer, and You have redeemed me from the hand of my enemy, the devil who comes to steal, to kill, and to destroy me with the contents within his hand, the curse, including sickness and disease. Because of You, I am delivered from the spirit of fear and from the power of death. I praise You because I am now free.

In Jesus' name, I give You all the glory, amen.

As an ambassador of Christ, how do the fruits of the Spirit aid me in supernatural healing? Turn to the next chapter to find out.

✝

SELF-EXAMINATION

Can I now identify the curse? Do I recognize when I am under attack by satan? Have I gained a greater understanding of Jesus, the Redeemer? Do I still harbor negative thoughts about God? Do I see Him as my redeemer, my source of help? If not, what steps do I need to take next?

NOTE

1. Becky Dvorak, *Greater than Magic* (Shippensburg, PA: Destiny Image Publishers, 2014), 59.

CHAPTER 4

✝

THE FRUITS OF AN AMBASSADOR TO HEAL

"I am an ambassador of Christ; as Jesus is, so am I on this earth. Like Him, I humbly walk in power of the fruits of the spirit—love, joy, peace, longsuffering, kindness, goodness, faithfulness, gentleness, and self-control. So that I can effectively carry out official kingdom business, such as to heal and be healed for His glory."

After an interview on the Christian radio station in Orange Walk, Belize, David and I walked into the lobby where we saw a number of sick people waiting and seeking assistance. We asked this tiny, elderly Mayan woman if we could pray for her, and she received healing in and throughout her physical body and could stand and walk without help, and all the arthritis pain was gone. As a result of her healing, she and the other family members who came with her received Jesus as their Savior.

Did you know that the moment you become born again you are automatically enlisted as an ambassador of Christ? You are chosen, predestined, and appointed by the King of kings, Jesus Himself, to carry out official kingdom business such as to heal and be healed for His glory. As His diplomat, you inherit His authority to conduct legitimate spiritual business in this world. You are endowed with supernatural power to bring about change for the good of the people around you. According to First John 4:17, you are entrusted to be like Jesus.

Also, you receive certification by the redemptive blood of Christ to deliver the Word of God with authority and to skillfully bring it to fruition, to manage delicate spiritual situations, and to handle people with His loving care.

Now then, we are ambassadors for Christ, as though God were pleading through us: we implore you on Christ's behalf, be reconciled to God (2 Corinthians 5:20).

THE NATURE OF CHRIST

If we are ambassadors of Christ on this earth, then we need to investigate the nature of His character so that we may represent Him correctly. Let's have a glimpse at just ten of His many qualities.

First of all, Jesus was humble and He came to serve, not to be served. He was not bound to a prideful spirit of entitlement. He was not about promoting Himself but His heavenly Father. In fact, He was able to minister to an individual just as if He was ministering to the multitudes. This humbleness that He chose made Him accessible to the people in need around Him. Philippians has this to report to us concerning Him:

Let this mind be in you which was also in Christ Jesus, who, being in the form of God, did not consider it robbery to be equal with God, but made Himself of no reputation, taking the form of a bondservant, and coming in the likeness of men. And being found in appearance as a man, He humbled Himself and became obedient to the point of death, even the death of the cross. Therefore God also has highly exalted Him and given Him the name which is above every name, that at the name of Jesus every knee should bow, of those in heaven, and of those

*on earth, and of those under the earth, and that every tongue
should confess that Jesus Christ is Lord, to the glory of God the
Father* (Philippians 2:5-11).

Can we lay aside a spirit of pride and the sin of entitlement? Does the
spotlight always have to shine on us? Or are we willing to give God the
glory? Are we content to be one of His servants? Or do we feel the need to
be "The Servant"? Do we make ourselves accessible to the lost and hurting
people around us? Or do we put ourselves above them? Are we truly able
to represent Him as He is, humble?

NINE CHARACTER TRAITS OF CHRIST

Let's look at nine more character traits of Christ, better known as the
fruits of the Spirit. They are *love, joy, peace, longsuffering, kindness, goodness, faithfulness, gentleness, and self-control* and are found in the apostle
Paul's writings in Galatians 5:22-23. And as we read through the four
gospels, Matthew, Mark, Luke, and John, we see that Jesus had to choose
to possess and activate these nine fruits of the Spirit on a daily basis. As
His ambassadors on this earth we need to do the same.

MAINTAIN A WELL-BALANCED DIET OF THE FRUITS OF THE SPIRIT

The fruits of the Spirit have been downplayed or even cast aside, and
the body of Christ is suffering because of it. Refusal to serve these fruits
has left many Christians malnourished and has allowed premature death
to set in to the spirit, soul, and physical body of the Church.

Obviously, we can't blame everything on the preachers in the pulpits.
There are faithful servants who are delivering a well-balanced diet of spiritual food to their congregants, but many of these congregants refuse to
partake of God's food. They no longer hunger and thirst after God and
are now anorexic in their faith.

Then we have bulimic Christians who gorge themselves on the Word
to make them feel good for the moment, but they have no desire to live

the lifestyle of Christ on a daily basis. So before the meeting is over or shortly thereafter, they've already vomited the feast of the Lord out from within them.

The fruits of the Spirit are necessary for maintaining a well-balanced spiritual diet. They build up our spiritual immune system so we can fight off the attacks of the enemy. They keep us strong in the faith.

Without them, sin will flourish and cause us to become mean, selfish, self-centered, and self-seeking. We will become weak in our faith, powerless in the Spirit, and eventually fall away from our Lord and His ways.

Love

Love is the greatest of all gifts and the most powerful fruit we can partake of. It empowers faith. Without love we cannot effectively release faith for the miraculous. Throughout the gospels we see that love motivates every miracle Jesus performs. He loves people unconditionally and puts the needs of others before Himself. Even when they beat, mock, and crucify Him, He still loves and forgives them. And because of His unconditional love His supernatural resurrection happens and the miraculous still takes place today.

Paul teaches us in Galatians 5:6, "*For in Christ Jesus neither circumcision nor uncircumcision has any value. The only thing that counts is faith expressing itself through love*" (NIV). Faith is not activated by legalism or by religious acts but by love alone. The Amplified version of the Bible puts it this way, "*For [if we are] in Christ Jesus neither circumcision nor uncircumcision means anything, but only faith activated and expressed and working through love*" (AMP).

God's definition and checklist of love are recorded in First Corinthians 13:4–8, "*Love suffers long and is kind; love does not envy; love does not parade itself, is not puffed up; does not behave rudely, does not seek its own, is not provoked, thinks no evil; does not rejoice in iniquity, but rejoices in the truth; bears all things, believes all things, hopes all things, endures all things. Love never fails.*"

Examine your heart. Is there any characteristic on love's checklist above that you need to work on? Remember, these attributes of love activate, energize, express, and work out faith for the miraculous. If you lack in the area of love, your faith is weak and ineffective. So strengthen your love today because faith operates by love. Your love level affects your ability to receive or release His healing power.

Joy

Joy is a supernatural force that gives us strength, and we are going to explore this more in-depth later on in the book. But because it is one of the nine fruits of the Spirit I want to take a brief look at it now as well.

I believe Jesus and joy go hand in hand together. Because it is a fruit of the Spirit of God, we need to guard our hearts from the negative ways of this world, and not allow its evil effects to bring us down and into a state of depression.

Let's face it, we live in a fallen world where things do go wrong. We all pass through difficult times, experience disappointment, and suffer hurt and pain from grief. But even though life can really hurt, it doesn't mean we have to remain in a permanent state of unhappiness. Just as we've been taught that love is a choice, so are joy and the other fruits of the Spirit for that matter.

I made a quality decision years ago that no matter what happens in this life I will always choose joy. Even if I have to hunt it down, I will find it. That doesn't necessarily mean I have to laugh all the time. But in all honesty, I probably laugh more than the average person. Why? Because I found the everlasting fruit of joy in Jesus, and He causes me to smile and laugh.

Sickness and disease and the pain and the stress they create can cause your joy level to go down, even diminish into depression. When you are fighting for your healing, you cannot afford to lose your joy. Nehemiah 8:10 digs up the ancient secret of supernatural strength. It reveals that, *"The joy of the Lord is your strength."* Joy helps in the healing process.

Peace

Peace is a state of being that is found in the presence of God. Philippians 4:6-7 exhorts us to, *"Be anxious for nothing, but in everything by prayer and supplication, with thanksgiving, let your requests be made known to God; and the peace of God, which surpasses all understanding, will guard your hearts and minds through Christ Jesus.*" Also, Second Timothy 1:7 tells us that God gave us a sound mind.

What is a sound mind? For one, it is a mind that is at peace. In regard to healing, it is one that determines that no matter what, it stays on Jesus and on His healing power. It rehearses not, over and over in the mind, the negative death report, but focuses on the abundant life found in Him.

If you are in a struggle with sickness and disease, spend more time with Jesus, who is full of peace and extends peace to those around Him. Then the cares and even the fears surrounding this sickness will relinquish their grip and will not be able to bind themselves to you. Your healing will be unleashed in His heavenly realm of peace.

Longsuffering

Longsuffering means to suffer long. In the New American Standard Version of the Bible, the word *longsuffering* is translated into the word *patience*, which is easier for most of us to understand. Patience is the ability to be able to wait peacefully when a situation is out of our natural control, without complaining or losing our temper or being consumed with worry, because the situation is taking longer than we would like.

Jesus is very patient with us. Second Peter 3:9 reveals an eternal benefit of being patient or longsuffering. It says, *"The Lord is not slow about His promise, as some count slowness, but is patient toward you, not wishing for any to perish but for all to come to repentance"* (NASB).

Nature provides us with an example of the benefits of being longsuffering or patient. In Guatemala we have a beautiful plant called the bird of paradise because the bloom looks like an exotic bird.

Once, a friend had planted one in his backyard, but after three years grew frustrated that it still had not bloomed. He lost his patience with it and was about to dig it up when his neighbor shared with him that with this plant he needed to exercise patience, because it takes anywhere from three to five years to bloom. Interestingly enough, it only blooms when the roots are under pressure, better known as *root bound*. He chose to be patient, and within the year reaped the harvest of a beautiful flower.

Okay, let's bring the importance of patience to a personal level concerning healing.

People are willing to wait seven to ten days for an antibiotic to heal their bodies because they have been taught for many years that if they take one spoonful or one tablet of this medicine three times a day, they will be healed. They are even willing to overlook physical symptoms of the illness because they have been taught that the symptoms and the sickness will be healed as long as they take the medicine faithfully. So their faith has been activated, they follow their doctor's instructions, and they are healed by the medicine.

But God's people are not willing to wait this amount of time for divine healing to manifest because they have not been taught that if they will be faithful to take God's medicine, His healing word, and exercise the power of patience their bodies will heal. Because of the lack of faith teaching for healing, if they experience any type of symptom after prayer they doubt the power in God's medicine and walk away from their healing.

When God's people hear the healing message and put faith for healing into action, they receive it. When taught consistently, they begin to walk in divine health and avoid sickness altogether.

I need to make one point very clear here. It is not us who wait patiently for God to heal because He gave healing to us already (see Isa. 53:4-5). He is patiently working with us according to our measure of faith. So we need to exercise patience with ourselves as we develop in our faith to believe for our healing. We should all be thankful that the Lord flourishes with longsuffering toward us as we learn to believe.

Kindness

Luke 6:35 gives us the real test of kindness. It challenges us to activate this fruit of the Spirit when the recipient is not kind to us. *"But love your enemies, and do good, and lend, expecting nothing in return; and your reward will be great, and you will be sons of the Most High; for He Himself is kind to ungrateful and evil men"* (NASB).

Oftentimes when people are sick and suffering with pain, their carnality overtakes them and they lack in the area of kindness. This is our opportunity to serve and dish out a heaping helping of kindness to them. It may take a while, but eventually they will respond in a positive manner. If we will persevere, it will help them to enter into the realm of kindness for themselves and partake of the other fruits of the Spirit, which will enable their faith to believe and trust God for healing too.

Wouldn't we desire unconditional kindness to help us overcome a difficult moment in our lives so that we can heal in spirit, in soul, and in body?

Goodness

Our God is sheer goodness. Remember when the Israelites were wandering in the desert for 40 years and how they complained and murmured about everything? God remained faithful and continued to pour out goodness upon them. He rained down fresh manna and provided fresh quail meat for them to eat; He quenched their thirst with water from the rock; their shoes and clothing did not wear out; He shielded them from the sun with the cloud by day, and guided and protected them by night with the pillar of fire. These are all acts of pure goodness. God wants us to acquire this character trait of His.

Psalm 136:1 admonishes us to be grateful, *"Oh, give thanks to the Lord, for He is good! For His mercy endures forever."*

God is good! As His ambassadors on this earth, we need to emanate His goodness to the lost and hurting people around us, even if these people are family members. A pure act of goodness goes a long way in the healing process. Ask the Lord today how you can show goodness to your spouse, mother, father, brother, sister, son, daughter, or other member of the family who is in need of healing.

Let's not forget that many people in today's world do not understand the meaning of goodness. It's never been demonstrated to them. So they only know how to lash out and act nasty when they are not well.

So again, ask the Holy Spirit to lead you to someone who is in need of a touch of His goodness. Then be willing to step out of your comfort zone and show them and tell them you care and, more importantly, how much the Lord cares for them. Be prepared to minister healing to them as the Lord reveals their needs to you.

Faithfulness

Faithfulness is not popular these days, but it is still a requirement of God for His people. It takes a decision from the heart to activate this fruit of the Spirit toward God, your spouse, your children, and other members of the family, your friends, your ministry, or your place of employment. It is often overlooked and unappreciated these days by others, but God is pleased when you activate this character trait of His. One day, you will hear Him say to you, *"Well done, good and faithful servant; you were faithful over a few things, I will make you ruler over many things. Enter into the joy of your lord"* (Matt. 25:21).

Can I add another area that you owe it to yourself to activate this fruit of the Spirit called faithfulness? Your healing journey to good health and well-being.

May I encourage you in your healing journey to start to confess *The Healing Creed* and remain faithful to speak this out loud at least once per day? As you remain faithful in this, you will start to take negative thoughts captive, and His healing promises will take root within your heart. Before you know it, you will hear yourself speak words of healing from your own mouth, your actions will begin to line up with these healing words, and soon your healing will begin to manifest.

Faithfulness in the little things of life always leads to bigger and greater things, such as the miraculous.

Gentleness

Let us not confuse gentleness with weakness. Gentleness is a strong character trait of the Lord that is not easy to obtain. In order for us to obtain this fruit of the Spirit, we have to allow the Holy Spirit to break our rebellious will.

Here is an example of this. We have two young horses that are being trained to ride. Before we can ride them we have to "gentle" them, meaning we have to break their wild behavior and teach them not to bite, buck, kick, or run away. They have to learn to be submissive and obedient to their master. We need to allow the Lord to gentle us as well.

> *The Lord's bond-servant must not be quarrelsome, but be kind to all, able to teach, patient when wronged, with gentleness correcting those who are in opposition, if perhaps God may grant them repentance leading to the knowledge of the truth, and they may come to their senses and escape from the snare of the devil, having been held captive by him to do his will* (2 Timothy 2:24–26 NASB).

Jesus is not weak when He walks the earth but strong in the fruit of gentleness as He submits to the will of the Father and offers His life in exchange for our redemption. As we emulate His gentleness, our rebellious nature will be broken, and we will become strong in the Spirit like He is, full of faith to believe for the miraculous.

Self-Control

Self-control is the ability to control one's emotions, behavior, and desires in order to obtain some reward later. This is an area that can be difficult for some to put under submission, especially women. We need to understand that faith is not an emotion but a foundation to stand upon when the proper feelings are not there.

Proverbs 16:32 instructs us in the area of self-control this way, *"He who is slow to anger is better than the mighty, and he who rules his spirit, than he who captures a city"* (NASB).

Jesus, under extreme and unjust circumstances, responded with complete self-control the night He was betrayed, arrested, and interrogated at an illegal trial, and the results of His self-control are that we are redeemed from satan and his curse of sickness and disease too.

To take your anger out on people or on God because you receive a bad report or you are not feeling good is not right. This fruit of the Spirit, self-control, will remind you to pull yourself together, to look at things truthfully, and remember that satan is the source of all wickedness including this sickness or disease.

It is so important to learn to activate the fruit of self-control so that the other fruits do not rot and your healing spoil. Keeping all the fruits of the Spirit fresh will fortify your faith to believe and receive your healing and miracle that you so long for.

THE ENEMY FEARS THE FRUITS OF THE SPIRIT

Not only do the fruits of the Spirit activate supernatural power, they also keep you healthier in spirit, in soul, and in body. The lack of them can prevent your faith from obtaining your miracle.

I often see people struggle to maintain the abundance of these fruits during the most critical moments of the battle between life and death. When someone needs to fight the hardest, the enemy fights overtime to get them to stumble in this area. Why? He's afraid of the supernatural power these fruits possess.

He's crafty in his ability to sidetrack us. This gives him the upper edge, so we drop our shield of faith against him and the spirit of premature death, and he can fire his most powerful weapons at us.

This doesn't mean you have to give in to his dirty war tactics. You have a free will. You can either enter into unnecessary battles or you can choose your battles wisely and stay focused and on the alert.

The battle plan of the enemy is to wear you down so you lose the desire to fight, give up, and die prematurely. So you see, how you tend to the fruits of the Spirit is important. When you do tend to them well, they will empower your faith to overcome and aid you in your supernatural healing.

HEALING TESTIMONY

Pain is a nasty weapon of satan, and it can cause us to struggle in the area of the fruits of the Spirit as well.

Police officer Les Cash from Buena Vista, Virginia about five or six years ago developed what is known to chiropractors as "cop back," or compressed disks in his lower spine that caused a lot of chronic pain. This pain made it difficult for him to stand after work and difficult to get out of bed in the morning. Let's hear from Les how he came to be healed.

> I met Becky through my wife, who had been healed by Jesus through Becky's hands about two years earlier. I went to a healing service, and she laid her hands on my back. And the people that were there said they actually saw me grow taller. After that meeting my back stopped hurting. I am able to get up out of bed without pain, I am able to train harder, work better, and move faster.
>
> This experience has furthered my walk with Jesus. I can't say enough about it. My back no longer hurts. About one year prior to my healing I had an x-ray to confirm that I did have compressed disks in my lower back. I don't need one now to confirm that the compressed disks are healed. I've got Jesus, I don't hurt anymore, I don't need anything else.

We will hear from his wife, Bridgete, in Chapter 9 as she shares her healing from temporomandibular joint disorder.

PRAYER

Dear Father God,

I admit, I do not fully understand what it means to be an ambassador of Christ, but I am willing to learn. Please teach me how to live a life that is worthy of this calling to represent You wherever I am and in whatever situation I face.

Forgive me for being prideful and for taking on this worldly sin of entitlement when all along You've asked me to be like Christ—a humble servant to the hurting and the lost.

Help me to effectively walk in the supernatural power of the fruits of Your spirit. I pray for the strength to be loving when others are not; to choose Your joy no matter what is happening around me; to live peacefully with those You place in my life; to understand the power of longsuffering to bring about a healing, whether this healing is for myself or for another; to show kindness instead of irritableness; and to exemplify Your goodness, especially to those who do not understand what goodness is.

My deepest desire is to remain faithful to You, Your Word, and to possess every faith-filled promise You have given every day of my life.

Remind me when I forget that gentleness is not a weakness, but Your strength working in me, and how important self-control is to my witness to a lost and dying world that is out of control so that I can effectively be about Your official kingdom business to heal and be healed for Your glory.

In Jesus' name I pray, amen.

Turn to the next chapter and learn how to activate the authority of Christ in your life so that you can overcome satan and all of his wicked attacks, including sickness and disease.

✝

SELF-EXAMINATION

As an ambassador of Christ, can I honestly say that I am His humble servant? Do I need to repent from the worldly sin of entitlement? Am I short on any of the fruits of the Spirit—love, joy, peace, longsuffering, kindness, goodness, faithfulness, gentleness, or self-control? Do I now understand the importance that these godly character traits possess in regard to obtaining my healing or supporting someone else for their healing?

CHAPTER 5

✝

THE AUTHORITY OF CHRIST

"I possess His authority over satan and all of his
wicked works, including sickness and disease.
Therefore, no weapon formed against me shall prosper,
nor will any plague come near my dwelling."

In this late day and hour, it's imperative that we possess a rock-solid revelation concerning our authority in Christ over satan and all of his wicked works. He gave to us, at the great price of His suffering, His authority to cast out demons, to heal the sick, and to overcome the power of darkness. Jesus encourages His followers with these words:

> *Listen carefully: I have given you authority [that you now possess] to tread on serpents and scorpions, and [the ability to exercise authority] over all the power of the enemy (Satan); and nothing will [in any way] harm you* (Luke 10:19 AMP).

He's given to us, by the power of His blood, His authority to tread or trample upon serpents and scorpions. This portion of Scripture does not refer to natural reptiles. We do have authority over these creatures as well (see Gen. 1:28). But He wants us to understand the message here—these

71

spiritual serpents and scorpions that Jesus is talking about are satan and demon spirits (Strong's, G3789).

Hopefully, this also brings clarification to the some of the Pentecostals who believe they have to prove their faith to others by handling poisonous snakes and drinking poisonous substances. This is just plain foolishness, and God's people perish, die, for a lack of knowledge concerning the Word (see Hos. 4:6). Even Jesus was tempted by the devil to do something deadly:

> Then he brought Him to Jerusalem, set Him on the pinnacle of the temple, and said to Him, "If You are the Son of God, throw Yourself down from here. For it is written: 'He shall give His angels charge over you, to keep you,' and, 'In their hands they shall bear you up, lest you dash your foot against a stone.'" And Jesus answered and said to him, "It has been said, 'You shall not tempt the Lord your God'" (Luke 4:9–12).

Loosely translated, Jesus responds to the devil and says, "Hey, you pressure Me to prove My faith in My God's faithfulness to protect Me. You say the only way I can prove that I believe is to throw Myself off from the pinnacle of the temple. I say, 'No!' I'm on to you, devil. You just want to kill Me so that I will not fulfill My destiny." And He says to us today, "You throw yourself off a tall building, you die before your appointed time. You play with poisonous snakes, they bite, and you die. You drink poison, you die. This is not how you prove your faith in My God's faithfulness. This is satan's wicked scheme to destroy you and your family. Use wisdom!"

We need to use our authority wisely; we are not in a battle against natural reptiles and human beings *but against principalities, against powers, against the rulers of the darkness of this age, against spiritual hosts of wickedness in the heavenly places* (Eph. 6:12). And First Peter 5:8 warns us to, *"Be sober, be vigilant; because your adversary the devil walks about like a roaring lion, seeking whom he may devour."* Jesus Christ gave us authority over all forces of evil. But so that you do know—yes, we indeed have authority over these natural poisonous creatures too. Here is a testimony to encourage your faith in case of an emergency situation.

Cynthia from Front Royal, Virginia was bitten by a brown recluse spider, but she took to heart the biblical healing messages in my books *Dare to Believe* and *Greater Than Magic* and put the power of the spoken word into action. She cursed the spider bite and commanded it to dry up and to disappear.

Jesus promises His followers in Luke 10:19, *"Behold, I give you the authority to trample on serpents and scorpions, and over all the power of the enemy, and nothing shall by any means hurt you."* No matter how the enemy tries to attack us to cause us harm, Jesus gives us His authority to overcome.

Later, she went to her doctor. He was amazed and took photos because he had never seen nor heard of a brown recluse spider bite heal on its own. They can take six months or more to heal with medication and often need surgical procedures such as scraping the poison out and skin grafts. She immediately testified of the healing power of Jesus Christ.

Again, Cynthia did not seek to get bitten; the creature bit her unaware. It was probably nesting in her clothing when she put them on.

WHEN DOES JESUS GIVE US HIS AUTHORITY?

When does Jesus do this for us, you wonder? When He allows His enemies to pierce His feet to the Cross of Calvary and bleeds so we can walk in His total authority on this earth over satan and all of his wicked works (see John 19:17–37).

It may be new news to some, but we do not need Christ's authority over the devil when we are in Heaven. He and his wicked troops are no longer allowed.

I should also add there is no sickness or disease or other form of the curse to fight off in Heaven. There's no temptation to overcome either, because there is no evil there. It is here on earth that we have been given His authority to overcome wickedness and the author of it, the devil.

AUTHORITY OVER SICKNESS AND DISEASE

Do Christians really have authority over sickness and disease? According to the Bible the answer to this question is yes, we really do. I want to teach you why we have authority over all sickness and disease.

To begin with, sickness and disease are made up of tiny living organisms called bacteria and viruses. What is the definition of an organism? "An individual form of life, such as a plant, animal, bacterium, protist, or fungus; a body made up of organs, organelles, or other parts that work together to carry on the various processes of life."[1]

Once, I asked the Lord for a simple explanation why we have authority over all sickness and disease. He answered me with the following vision and Scripture.

I saw myself looking into a microscope, and on the plate of glass being examined were sickness and disease. The Lord asked me to tell Him what I saw. I told Him that I saw them moving. He explained to me that is because sickness and disease are made up of microscopic living organisms that move and get inside the body and make people sick.

He then gave me the following verse from Genesis 1:28: "*Then God blessed them, and God said to them, 'Be fruitful and multiply; fill the earth and subdue it; have dominion over the fish of the sea, over the birds of the air, and over every living thing that moves on the earth.'*"

According to this verse we have been given dominion over everything that lives and moves on this earth, including sickness and disease. To dominate means to control, govern, or rule by superior authority or power. He has given us dominion over these tiny microscopic organisms.

What about bacteria?

Bacteria are organisms made up of just one cell. They are capable of multiplying by themselves, as they have the power to divide. Their shapes vary, and doctors use these characteristics to separate them into groups.

Bacteria exist everywhere, inside and on our bodies. Most of them are completely harmless and some of them are very useful. But some can cause disease, either because they end up in the wrong place in the body or simply because they are "designed" to invade us.[2]

Ponder upon this phrase concerning harmful bacteria for a while: "designed to invade us." Spiritually speaking this sounds like a weapon of warfare. What does God's Word say about weapons that are formed to harm us? It says, *"No weapon formed against you shall prosper"* (Isa. 54:17.) Our Lord promises us that these weapons formed against us, including harmful bacteria, shall not prosper.

What about a virus?

A virus is "an ultramicroscopic (20 to 300 nanometers in diameter), metabolically inert, infectious agent that replicates only within the cells of living hosts, mainly bacteria, plants, and animals: composed of an RNA or DNA core, a protein coat, and, in more complex types, a surrounding envelope."[3]

Did you notice in the definition that a virus is called an infectious agent? Again, this is something to cause us harm. According to James 1:17 God does not give us things that will harm us. It says, *"Every good gift and every perfect gift is from above, and comes down from the Father of lights, with whom there is no variation or shadow of turning."* Let me remind you what Jesus says in John 10:10, just who these things come from. *"The thief does not come except to steal, and to kill, and to destroy. I have come that they may have life, and that they may have it more abundantly."* Remember, the thief is satan and he uses his weapons of sickness and disease to harm us. God does not give us infectious agents.

Science teaches us that there are different types of infectious agents in many shapes and sizes. Bacteria and protozoa are microscopic one-celled organisms, while viruses are even smaller. Fungi grow like plants, and helminths resemble worms.[4]

What hope does the Lord give us concerning these infectious agents? He says in Luke 10:19, *"Behold, I give you the authority to trample on serpents and scorpions, and over all the power of the enemy, and nothing shall by any means hurt you."*

Three Reasons We Have Authority over Sickness and Disease:

1.   He gives us dominion over all living things on this earth, including microscopic organisms that can make us sick.

2.   God promises us that weapons formed against us, including harmful bacteria designed to invade us, shall not prosper.

3.   Jesus Christ gives to us all authority over satan and his wicked works, including infectious agents called viruses.

No Weapon Formed Against Us Shall Prosper

Our enemy the devil has fashioned many weapons to use against us, but we are not helpless against him. Remember, God has given you His authority over satan and all of his wicked works, including sickness and disease.

Monica Atkins from Lexington, Virginia was diagnosed in 2013 with a chronic eye infection called blepharitis. In her words, this is what she had to deal with on a daily basis.

> About two years ago I started having another issue with my eyes or technically my eyelids! I was diagnosed with a condition called blepharitis, which is a chronic infection of the eyelids that causes extreme burning and redness of the eyes due to discharge that secretes from the eyelids. Every day I would experience intense burning in my eyes throughout the day that basically felt like acid was being poured into my eyes. My eyes would sting and burn anytime my eyes watered. Anytime I teared up or cried!

My doctor prescribed eye drops and an eye cream that was almost like Vaseline that I would have to apply daily to try to help alleviate the burning and redness. I had to use daily eye washes with baby shampoo and special solutions, but none of this was a cure and it only helped to stop the burning at times. I searched the Internet for "cures" and natural remedies. I tried everything from warm compresses to salt water flushes to "blink" therapy but nothing worked! I would carry antibacterial wipes (which you are to never use on your eyes according to the warning labels) because those would actually temporarily stop the burning sensation for a while.

I began to just live with the discomfort of this eye infection and make accommodations that would get me through the day.

If only the local church would wake up and teach people they can be free from sickness and disease, God's people would not have to suffer from satan's weapons. As true ambassadors we need to be willing to impart His healing message to others. Whether it is to a special healing service at a nearby church or just a casual gathering in your home, invite them, tell them, pray for them.

Back in 2013, Monica's friend invited her to come to a special healing service in a nearby town. What was interesting was that she had just listened to a pastor preach a sermon about healing on a podcast. This pastor shared a story about a missionary from Guatemala who had a children's home and prayed for the children and saw them healed. He continued to share other healing testimonies about this woman's ministry, like the deaf hearing. So it caught her attention when her friend invited her to a healing service and the healing minister was a missionary from Guatemala who had a children's home there and saw the children healed.

The Holy Spirit was wooing Monica to come to a healing service and was confirming the healing minister with her. That's a personal invite from the Lord Himself to come and taste the goodness of the Lord.

So Monica accepted her friend's invite, and she heard a message about the redemptive blood of Jesus Christ to heal us in spirit, in soul, and in body. Not only did the healing message resonate within her spirit but she saw with her own eyes people being healed. Just like the pastor on the podcast shared, she witnessed the deaf hear and other types of healing as well. The Holy Spirit caught her attention and her spiritual eyes began to open, but it all started with an invite from an ambassador of Christ.

Two years passed since that first healing service. It was now November of 2015, and again another invitation came from this same friend to attend a healing service in her area. She accepted. Again, she heard a message of faith that stirred her spirit, but this time she believed for her own healing. She activated her faith, received a healing touch, and her eyes were completely healed in a moment of time. She no longer had to put up with blepharitis. She was free from excruciating, burning pain in her eyes. No longer did she need to go through the tedious routine of cleansing her eyelids or use prescribed drops and creams or figure out alternative ways to find some relief just to get through the day. God gave her everything she needed to overcome these spiritual attacks. Her eyes were healed in the name of Jesus.

There are times when the enemy is persistent. He will look for a weak link to pry his way back into our life. He tried this with Monica. Why? Because he was afraid of the eternal results healing produces.

You see, Monica is also a true ambassador of Jesus Christ, and she regularly shares her faith with others. She openly testifies of the goodness of God in her life, like the healing of her eyes.

Now, I know what some of you reading this are thinking already, "Well, then I am not going to speak to anyone of my healing if satan is going to try to steal it from me." Wrong thinking!

That's what he wants you to do because he witnessed that there is the power of life and death in the tongue, and as we will share later on, this is one of the weapons you use to solidify your healing. Remember, another spiritual weapon Elohim gives to us is His authority over the devil and his evil works.

One way the enemy attacks us is when we are unaware of his tactics. You know, we are naïve to think that he will not try to put the same disease upon us again. He will try to destroy our credibility by stealing our healing if we will let him.

We can look at the wickedness of the terrorists today for an example of how satan works. (If we don't know, satan is the one inspiring these spiritually sick souls.) Anyway, they look for a soft target and maliciously attack to destroy them. But they don't stop with this first attack; they look for another weak target and attack again with the same method of destruction until we do what we need to do and strengthen the weak link. To keep with the message of this book, we need to strengthen our faith for healing. The serpent of old, the devil, is the mastermind of terrorism, and he terrorizes people with hideous forms of suffering with sickness and disease.

This leads us to another spiritual weapon God has given to us to overcome satan's weapons formed against us—faith in action. With this weapon, we take the Word of God and speak aloud its promises. But we do not stop there; we put action behind our words. If we speak we are healed, then we must act like we are healed. No matter if this is the first attack or the second, we must activate our faith-filled words with our action.

Back to Monica's testimony. For her employment, she worked on a computer all day. Some days, she felt tired in the eyes. She just needed a break, but the enemy took advantage and tried to put fear on her and remind her of the pain with familiar symptoms.

For a brief moment, she thought, "Oh no, it wants to come back!" But immediately she realized this was an attack—just an attack. She remembered her authority in Christ and refused to allow these lying symptoms access into her eyes again. The enemy acknowledged her authority over him, backed off, and the symptoms left and she was free and whole.

You see, our enemy has many different types of weapons that he fashions to use against us. Sickness and disease are part of his weaponry.

They are deadly to us if we do not recognize them as satan's weapons and accept them.

God has given us greater spiritual weapons to use to defend ourselves while under attack. Better yet, these weapons can ward off these wicked attacks.

WHAT ARE SOME OF OUR SPIRITUAL WEAPONS?

1. The Holy Spirit
2. The authority of the believer in Christ Jesus
3. The power of the spoken word
4. Faith in action
5. God's healing message found in the Holy Bible

NO PLAGUES SHALL COME NEAR YOU

In these last days there is an increase of horrific plagues and pestilences; the Bible warns us of these things. In Matthew 24:7 it says, *"For nation will rise against nation, and kingdom against kingdom. And there will be famines, pestilences, and earthquakes in various places."* This same warning is repeated in Luke 21:10-11. In these last days there will be an increase of incurable pestilences and plagues. The fourth seal recorded in the Book of Revelation prophecies:

> *I looked, and behold, an ashen horse; and he who sat on it had the name Death; and Hades was following with him. Authority was given to them over a fourth of the earth, to kill with sword and with famine and with pestilence and by the wild beasts of the earth* (Revelation 6:8 NASB).

This word *pestilence* comes from the Greek word *loimos* and means a plague—literally, the disease; or figuratively, a pest (Strong's G3061). The definition of the word *plague* comes from the Hebrew word *nega'* and it means an infliction like a mark or spot, sore, wound from a disease or a disease itself, like leprosy (Strong's H5061).

With these prophesies and others from God's Word, our gracious Savior and Lord is warning us to prepare for the days ahead of us. We need to understand how to function as an ambassador of Christ and activate His healing power, not just for ourselves and for our personal family members but for the benefit of others as well. We need to make ready ourselves spiritually so that we can activate this promise from Psalm 91:10, *"Nor shall any plague come near your dwelling."*

PROTECTION FOR MOSES AND THE ISRAELITES

Looking back into history, we read about how Moses and the Israelites were protected from the ten plagues that fell upon Pharaoh and the Egyptians. (Read Exodus 7 through 12.)

After reading the account of these horrific plagues, there are a few points that stand out to me more than others. First, God gave warning to the rebellious pharaoh and to the Egyptians what was going to come upon them if they did not heed Him. Second, even though God's people were living in the midst of the plagues and pestilences, He provided a plan of protection for His people.

Let's zero in on the tenth plague; this is where the spirit of death was to take the life of the firstborn from every household unless they painted the two doorposts of their home with the blood of a lamb.

> *For I will pass through the land of Egypt on that night, and will strike all the firstborn in the land of Egypt, both man and beast; and against all the gods of Egypt I will execute judgment: I am the Lord. Now the blood shall be a sign for you on the houses where you are. And when I see the blood, I will pass over you; and the plague shall not be on you to destroy you when I strike the land of Egypt* (Exodus 12:12-13).

How appropriate and prophetic is this portion of Scripture for us today. Because we live under a new covenant, we no longer have to slaughter a lamb and paint our doorposts with its blood for protection. Jesus is our sacrificial lamb, and by His shed blood we are redeemed from this spirit of death that will try to steal, to kill, and to destroy us.

We have a promise to stand upon, *"No harm befalls the righteous, but the wicked are filled with trouble"* (Prov. 12:21 NASB). As with every other promise of God, we need to know how to activate the power of the promise. In this case, this promise is for the righteous, or those who are justified or vindicated by God. Today, the only way we can be justified or vindicated by God is through the atonement of Jesus Christ. (See Chapter 3.)

We need to make this point clear—just because Jesus shed His blood for us already for our redemption does not mean we do not have a part to play in our protection against plagues and pestilences. The opposite is true. We are responsible to activate the power of the blood in our lives.

THE RESPONSIBILITY IS IN OUR HANDS

There comes a point when the responsibility is in our hands, as we find out in the story of Moses and the Israelites. The Pharaoh and his army are in hot pursuit of Moses and the sons of Israel. They find them camped in front of the sea. The people fill with fear as their enemy draws near. They begin to shout sarcastic remarks at Moses. But Moses, the mighty man of faith, responds to the people. He says:

> *Do not fear! Stand by and see the salvation of the Lord which He will accomplish for you today; for the Egyptians whom you have seen today, you will never see them again forever. The Lord will fight for you while you keep silent* (Exodus 14:13-14 NASB).

His response sounds so right on, but the Lord teaches Moses and us that there comes a time when mere words are not enough. There must be action behind our words, and we are the ones responsible to take action. Listen to the Lord's response to Moses' valiant statement of faith.

> *Then the Lord said to Moses, "Why are you crying out to Me? Tell the sons of Israel to go forward. As for you, lift up your*

staff and stretch out your hand over the sea and divide it" (Exodus 14:15-16 NASB).

This is an intense moment for these people. In fact, it is a life and death situation for them, and the Lord says to Moses to stop crying and tell the people to move forward! And He doesn't stop there. He tells Moses that he is to put his faith into action and divide the Red Sea.

All too often, we expect the Lord to do the supernatural for us. But as we study the Word, we see that the Lord has a different plan. He provides everything we need to succeed. Then He expects us to be responsible and not just speak words of faith but put action behind our faith-filled words and divide our own Red Seas by the supernatural power of our faith in the redemptive work of Jesus. He places the responsibility into our hands.

PRAYER

Dear Jesus,

How we thank You that You gave to us Your authority to walk on this earth when they nailed Your precious feet to the Cross and You bled. We do not take this authority lightly, nor will we toss it aside as if it has no value.

On the contrary, the power of Your blood that You shed gives us victory in every situation satan tries to throw at us. No more are we in bondage to his wicked attacks such as sickness, disease, plagues, and pestilences. We are free from every weapon he forms against us. We gladly possess Your authority.

In Your name we rejoice, amen!

Did you forget about God's benefits? Turn to the next chapter for a refresher course. If you never heard of them before, learn what they are and how they truly can make all the difference in your life.

✝

SELF-EXAMINATION

Are you beginning to understand your authority as a believer in Christ Jesus? Do you sense His protection over you and your family, knowing now that you possess authority over sickness, disease, plagues, and pestilences? Are you ready to activate the authority of Christ in the present situation that you face?

NOTES

1. *American Heritage® Dictionary of the English Language,* Fifth Edition, s.v. "organism," accessed May 16, 2016, http://www .thefreedictionary.com/organism.

2. Flemming Andersen, "Viruses and Bacteria," Netdoctor, February 05, 2014, http://www.netdoctor.co.uk/health_advice/facts/ virusbacteria.htm.

3. Dictionary.com, Dictionary.com Unabridged, Random House, Inc. s.v. "virus," accessed May 16, 2016, http://www.dictionary.com/ browse/virus.

4. "Types of Infectious Agents," Mayo Clinic, accessed May 16, 2016, http://www.mayoclinic.org/diseases-conditions/infectious-diseases/ multimedia/types-of-infectious-agents/img-20008643.

CHAPTER 6

✝

REMEMBER ALL OF HIS BENEFITS

"I bless the sweet Lamb of God; I remember all of His benefits, who pardons all iniquities, heals all disease, redeems my life from destruction, crowns me with lovingkindness and tender mercies, satisfies my mouth with good things, and renews my youth like the eagle's."

We are to bless the Lord. This word *bless* comes from the Hebrew word *barak*, which means to kneel down in adoration, praise, and thanksgiving (Strong's, H1288). When is the last time we got down on our knees before the Lord and worshiped Him for all the good things He has done for us? Or have we taken on the world's negative mindset and only see the bad in life and forget about the good things that come from God? Seriously, we bless Elohim when we count our blessings from Him, and we also strengthen the power of His goodness in our lives when we verbalize His good deeds with our words.

To kneel before the Lord is to humble ourselves before Him. In other words, we lift Him up by lowering ourselves. We acknowledge His greatness and our dependence upon Him.

When we bless Him, we fix our eyes on Him and not on the negative situations that confront us. Satan and his powers of darkness, like sickness and disease, lose their stronghold over us.

It encourages our faith, especially when we feel down or afraid, to take the time to remember all the many ways God blesses us and intervenes on our behalf. In Exodus 15, Moses and the sons of Israel sing a powerful song of praise and adoration about the mighty ways God delivers them from the hand of their enemies.

If you're like most Christians, you have not been taught how to worship the Lord properly. Find a quiet and private place; remember, humble yourself and kneel before Him. From your heart, bless Him with your words. Use the Scriptures to start with, like the words from Psalm 103:1, *"Bless the Lord, O my soul; and all that is within me, bless His holy name!"* Continue on from there.

When I bless Him, I personalize nuggets of Scripture that remind me of His goodness toward me. For example, "You are the reason that I live. You are the very breath that I breathe. Your joy is my strength. When I feel weak, You remain strong. You are faithful and true. You never change; You are the same yesterday, today, and forever. By Your stripes I am healed." Then with my own words I start to praise Him for all that He is doing in my life today.

You can be certain of this—the more you practice blessing the Lord, the easier it will become. He will work with you to find your way. The main point is that it comes from your heart.

REMEMBER ALL OF HIS BENEFITS

The Scriptures remind us to forget not all of His benefits. But first, we have to know what His benefits are in order to remember to activate them in our lives. Psalms so beautifully describes what His benefits are:

Bless the Lord, O my soul, and forget not all His benefits: who forgives all your iniquities, who heals all your diseases, who redeems your life from destruction, who crowns you with lovingkindness and tender mercies, who satisfies your mouth with good things, so that your youth is renewed like the eagle's (Psalm 103:2–5).

1.   He forgives our iniquities.

2.   He heals all our diseases.

3.   He redeems our life from destruction.

4.   He crowns us with lovingkindness and tender mercies.

5.   He satisfies our mouth with good things.

6.   He renews our youth like the eagle's.

HE PARDONS ALL INIQUITIES

In Him we have redemption through His blood, the forgiveness of sins, according to the riches of His grace which He made to abound toward us in all wisdom and prudence, having made known to us the mystery of His will, according to His good pleasure which He purposed in Himself, that in the dispensation of the fullness of the times He might gather together in one all things in Christ, both which are in heaven and which are on earth—in Him (Ephesians 1:7–10).

God is faithful and true, and as we discussed earlier He forgives our iniquities, our perversity, and our sin. The following is a beautiful testimony of forgiveness.

A divorced man with seven daughters was given a chance to help his daughters start to heal emotionally from years of pain that he caused them, but he struggled within himself to make the right choice. Convinced they would never believe him, he was afraid that his daughters would not accept his apology.

He also struggled to forgive himself. We shared with him the power of Jesus Christ to forgive and to release us from all unrighteousness. We gave him the opportunity to make his life right with Jesus. He accepted the offer and prayed and asked the Father to forgive him and asked Jesus to be his Savior.

We began to explain to the man about his daughters' need to hear him apologize to them so that they could start to heal. Without his sincere words of sorrow for the pain his iniquities caused, they would have a very difficult life. We asked him if this was what he wanted for them.

As sincere tears flowed from his eyes, he asked each one of his girls to come to him. He tenderly looked each one in the eye and asked them to forgive him. Each one fell into his arms and cried from the depths of their hearts.

This man made the right choice—he asked for the Lord to forgive him for his wickedness and then asked his daughters to forgive him as well. The Lord knew the sincerity of this man's heart and pardoned his iniquities, his perversity, and his sin.

He Heals All Disease

Many Christians wonder if God still heals today. Yes, He does. Just like He still forgives our iniquities and offers eternal life to those who believe. Hebrews 13:8 reassures us that Jesus Christ *is* the same yesterday, today, and forever. The Lord does not retract physical healing from His blood covenant.

He heals all disease—not just some disease, but all. When we activate His authority in us, every illness must surrender and leave our bodies in His name.

Jeremiah 32:17 declares, "*Ah, Lord God! Behold, You have made the heavens and the earth by Your great power and outstretched arm. There is nothing too hard for You.*"

He Redeems Our Life from Destruction

He has delivered us from the power of darkness and conveyed us into the kingdom of the Son of His love, in whom we have redemption through His blood, the forgiveness of sins (Colossians 1:13-14).

There are many forms of destruction that the devil uses to destroy us if we let him. One of these spiritual weapons is addiction, and it causes mass destruction.

So many of God's people are in bondage to addictive behaviors; they want to be free but don't know how. One such young woman came forward for ministry at a healing conference in Kentucky. Her addiction was cigarettes and it had control over her. She wanted deliverance and freedom. I laid hands upon her and renounced the spirit of addiction in her and declared that from now on when she would try to smoke a cigarette she would start to vomit. She put it to the test. As soon as the service was over she ran outside and took a puff of a cigarette and her body immediately started to vomit on the church steps. Her body now rejected what it once craved. But along with physical deliverance, her soul, mind, and emotions needed to be healed and renewed to remain free from the addiction.

You may be like this woman, with an addiction to some type of sinful behavior, and need deliverance and renewal of your mind. Here is a plan of action from the Scriptures to help you overcome any and all addictive behaviors.

1. Before you can overcome an addiction, you first have to admit that you have a problem and that it is a sin. James 5:16 instructs us to, *"Confess your sins to one another, and pray for one another so that you may be healed. The effective prayer of a righteous man can accomplish much"* (NASB).

2. Make a quality decision that you will do whatever is necessary to be free from this ungodly behavior. There is a plan to freedom in James 4:7, *"Therefore submit to God. Resist the devil and he will flee from you."*

How do you submit to God and resist the devil?

* Ask God for forgiveness. *"If we confess our sins, He is faithful and just to forgive us our sins and to cleanse us from all unrighteousness"* (1 John 1:9).

* Read the Bible and cleanse yourself spiritually. *"That He might sanctify and cleanse her with the washing of water by the word"* (Eph. 5:26).

* Listen to faith building messages. *"So then faith comes by hearing, and hearing by the word of God"* (Rom. 10:17).

* Fast and pray for deliverance. *"So He said to them, 'This kind can come out by nothing but prayer and fasting'"* (Mark 9:29).

* Pray in the Spirit to encourage yourself. *"But you, beloved, building yourselves up on your most holy faith, praying in the Holy Spirit"* (Jude 1:20).

* Take control of your thoughts. *"Casting down arguments and every high thing that exalts itself against the knowledge of God, bringing every thought into captivity to the obedience of Christ"* (2 Cor. 10:5).

* Confess out loud the promises of God over yourself. *"Death and life are in the power of the tongue, and those who love it will eat its fruit"* (Prov. 18:21).

* Keep your joy level strong. *"Do not sorrow, for the joy of the Lord is your strength"* (Neh. 8:10).

* Be full of the Holy Spirit. *"And do not be drunk with wine, in which is dissipation; but be filled with the Spirit, speaking to one another in psalms and hymns and spiritual songs, singing and making melody in your heart to the Lord,*

giving thanks always for all things to God the Father in the name of our Lord Jesus Christ" (Eph. 5:18–20).

* Don't take on stress or worry; give it to God. *"Be anxious for nothing, but in everything by prayer and supplication, with thanksgiving, let your requests be made known to God"* (Phil. 4:6).

* Surround yourself with supportive people who will hold you accountable to your actions. *"Do not be deceived: 'Evil company corrupts good habits'"* (1 Cor. 15:33).

A spirit of addiction is out to control and destroy you. To be free from the powers of darkness, you have to make a quality decision that you will do whatever it takes to be delivered from its destructive power. If you will do these things on a daily basis, eventually you will break free from sinful and addictive behaviors. The enemy will flee from you, and the freedom you so desire will be yours.

CROWNED WITH LOVINGKINDNESS AND TENDER MERCIES

Remember Monica's miraculous healing from the incurable eye disease, blepharitis? Well, she had been diagnosed with another eye disease that in the natural realm has no known cure. But does this earthly fact stop God's healing power? No, it does not. Actually, it sets you up for a miracle, because without an impossible situation you cannot have a miracle.

In 2004, Monica was diagnosed with Adie's tonic pupil, or Adie syndrome, which is a rare neurological condition that affects the pupil of the eye. This eye disease can affect people in different ways, but in her situation she woke up one morning and one of her pupils was very large and the other one was very small. Her pupils would not respond correctly to light. They would not dilate or constrict with light changes as they were created to do.

She says, "I was most affected by extreme sensitivity to the sun and to florescent lights because my pupils would not constrict in light as a normal pupil would. At night I had difficulty adjusting to change from light to dark because sometimes my pupils would be very small and would not dilate in the dark so it made it harder to see when driving at night or even walking around in darker settings."

She learned a bad spiritual habit that many of God's people do. She learned to live with this condition and adjusted her lifestyle to accommodate it for over ten years. That is a decade of unnecessary suffering from the devil.

However, since she exercised her faith and was healed from blepharitis one year ago, she realized that something else had taken place since then. I want you to hear this part of Monica's testimony from her own words.

> But what is interesting is that I have started to notice that my eyes aren't so sensitive to light these days. I can see in the dark better! My pupils have started to act normal! Not only have I been healed of the blepharitis infection, but this healing from Adie's tonic pupil kind of snuck up on me, and as suddenly as these conditions appeared, they disappeared! I have no symptoms at all of the Adie syndrome now! I can see better in the dark. I don't have to wear sunglasses in the rain! It's crazy! It's the coolest thing ever!

This, to me, is a prime example of God crowning us with His lovingkindness and tender mercies. Monica was suffering for years with this eye disease and became so accustomed to it that she didn't even think to receive healing for it because the acid-like burning sensation in her eyes from the other disease, blepharitis, had her attention day in and day out. But God knew.

The moment she was crowned with His lovingkindness and tender mercy is the day she inherited all the jewels He possessed, including healing from Adie's syndrome.

HE FILLS OUR MOUTHS WITH GOOD THINGS

A good man out of the good treasure of his heart brings forth good; and an evil man out of the evil treasure of his heart brings forth evil. For out of the abundance of the heart his mouth speaks (Luke 6:45).

The heart and the mouth are powerful instruments in the realm of faith. The mouth proclaims what is in the depths of the spiritual heart. Romans 10:8–10 confirms this and gives deeper insight to their purpose:

"The word is near you, in your mouth and in your heart" (that is, the word of faith which we preach): that if you confess with your mouth the Lord Jesus and believe in your heart that God has raised Him from the dead, you will be saved. For with the heart one believes unto righteousness, and with the mouth confession is made unto salvation.

According to this portion of Scripture, the heart believes and the mouth confesses. What does the heart believe? It believes unto righteousness—justification or right standing with God. And what does the heart confess? Confession is made unto salvation, and according to our word study in Chapter 2 this word *salvation* is holistic and includes healing of the spirit, soul, and body.

In Psalm 103:2–5, one of the benefits we are to remember is that He satisfies our mouths with good things. We are to take these good things and impart them to others, like faith for eternal life with Jesus, faith for deliverance from demonic oppression or possession, or faith for physical healing to name a few of the good things.

Let's focus in on the spiritual purpose of the mouth in regard to physical healing. Now, the devil does not want us to share these good things with others. In fact, he is downright nasty, and he wants us to keep quiet about the glory of our Lord. One way he will try to gag us is with physical weapons of sickness and disease against the mouth. It is a challenge to be a mouthpiece for the Lord when your mouth is swollen or full of sores or inflicted with some other type of illness. It makes it laborious to speak out loud when the mouth is sick.

Last year, a couple of days before I would minister, my tongue would break out with canker sores. At first, I thought it was because I was dehydrated from the plane ride, and from a human standpoint it was a logical explanation. The second time it happened, I started to wonder if this was spiritual and not physical because I made sure I drank plenty of water before, during, and after the flight. The third time it happened, I knew without a doubt I was under attack.

To break this demonic attack against the power of my tongue, my good friend Palma and I entered into a time of prayer and fasting. The stronghold was broken, and I did not have this problem again.

Another minister, Margie from Ocala, Florida, suffered from severe gum disease. She could not eat or even touch her teeth lightly together without serious pain. But the message she heard taught at the healing service resonated deep within her spirit, and she put the message of faith to the test and activated her faith. She started to bite down on her teeth. To Margie's delight, her gums and teeth were instantly healed in Jesus' name.

No matter how we were attacked by the enemy, we continued to confess with our mouths what we believed in our hearts to be true about the goodness of the Lord's salvation to the people. When we were in need, we both received supernatural healing in our mouths as well.

> *I have not hid thy righteousness within my heart; I have declared thy faithfulness and thy salvation: I have not concealed thy lovingkindness and thy truth from the great congregation* (Psalm 40:10 KJV).

HE RENEWS OUR YOUTH LIKE THE EAGLE'S

I saw posted on social media the other day a photo of an elderly woman pushed off a cliff by her daughter. The caption threatened that if you were not kind to your daughter now, she might not be so kind to you later on when you need her help. After all, you are aging, weakening, falling apart, depreciating in value to the world, and with your negative thoughts and confessions you are binding yourself to a wheelchair.

Again, we have bought into another lie of the devil and believe that as we age we need to fall apart, as if we are bound to the curse. God's promise to us is the opposite; He vows that He will renew our youth like the eagle's. But we are responsible to activate this supernatural renewal from our heavenly Father.

Once, after a time of ministry in Florida I was taken on a tour of the area and brought to a natural wildlife park. As we drove through the park, the ranger stopped us and asked us to come look into his telescope to observe a juvenile eagle that just returned from his first flight.

This young juvenile was muscular, full of vigor and strength. It jumped up and down, and its wings flapped with excitement from the new experience of flight. It was eager to fly again.

This is the image that God wants us to have as we enter into our elderly years. He desires to renew our strength from all the years of hard work. It is not His will that we are full of pain and suffering, that we are too weak to enjoy life, or that we give up all together and complain and tell everyone that we just want to die and go home to be with the Lord.

God's Word tells us that this is the day that He has made, and that we are to rejoice and be glad in it (see Ps. 118:24). The reason you are still on this earth is that He still has things for you to accomplish for His glory. It does not bless the Lord when we will to die. No, we need to press into His will, activate healing, and discover His purpose for our last days on this earth.

"Yes, Jesus wants to heal that too!" This is my response to an elderly woman who bursts out with joy as all the arthritis pain is instantly gone from her husband. In response to her request, I place my hands over his ears and he can instantly hear out of his once deaf ears. Then he asks me to minister to his weak eyes, and they too renew like in the days of his youth. Jesus wants to restore our youth!

At another meeting, an elderly woman steps forward for healing of various ailments. The main healing she desires is for her digestive system.

She is always in great pain because her intestines cramp into a ball. This causes severe pain and discomfort. This situation controls her everyday life.

I release the healing power of the Holy Spirit into her body she shouts out that she feels as if a baby is moving within her as her intestines release and move back into place.

This precious elderly woman also suffers from arthritis all over her body, and all the pain just lifts off of her body. She also suffers from tinnitus and the ringing ceases instantly in the name of Jesus. Her testimony blesses the entire congregation as she stands and declares the goodness of our Lord over her.

Regardless of age, healing belongs to those of us who believe in the healing power of Jesus Christ. He deeply desires to renew our youth, so much so that He shed His blood for our physical renewal when they whipped Him for all sickness, all disease, all pain, all suffering, and for all symptoms.

It's time for us to remember all of His benefits, who pardons all iniquities, heals all diseases, redeems us from destruction, crowns us with lovingkindness and tender mercies, satisfies our mouths with good things, and renews our youth like the eagle's.

PRAYER

Dear Father God,

Forgive us; we have strayed away from the truth of Your word. We even forgot about Your benefits, and because of it we have suffered needlessly.

Today we kneel down in adoration before You because our faith has been restored. We now remember all of Your benefits. You pardon all our iniquities, our perversities, and our sins. You heal us from all disease. You redeem us from destruction. You crown us with Your lovingkindness and tender mercies. You satisfy our mouths with good things that we can impart to others, and You renew our strength like the eagle's.

We have much to be grateful for. Thank You for all Your benefits.
In Jesus' name, we praise as we pray, amen.

Are you secure in your faith that God is indeed willing and able to heal you in spirit, in soul, and in body? Let's turn to the next chapter and find out why we can be sure of this.

✝

SELF-EXAMINATION

Do I take time to bless the Lord for all He has done for me? Am I able to bow down before Him in private worship? How about in public worship? Am I willing to start to bless the Lord in this way? Did I forget about His benefits? Will I remember all of His benefits from this day forward? Have I asked Him to pardon me of all my iniquities, perversities, and sins? Do I need Him to heal a sickness or disease? Am I willing to activate this benefit of healing in my life? Have I allowed Him to redeem my life from all forms of destruction? Or am I holding on to some addictions that I need to be free from? Will I allow Him to crown me with His lovingkindness and tender mercies? Will I allow Him to satisfy my mouth with His good bounty to share with others? Am I ready to rid myself from the world's negative prospect of aging? Will I receive His renewal of my youth like the eagle's.

CHAPTER 7

✝

ABLE AND WILLING TO HEAL

"I am grateful that You are both able and willing to heal me in spirit, soul, and body. I partake of Your bread of life, and drink from the cup of Your New Covenant to restore health to me and to heal me of my wounds with Your healing balm of Gilead."

I am so grateful for the healing power of Jesus Christ to heal us in every area of life. I praise Him not only because He is capable to heal, but He yearns for His healing power to manifest within me as well.

Perhaps you are not to this point in your faith walk yet to praise Him for supernatural healing. Maybe you still have some unanswered questions concerning God's will to heal. May I suggest that you read on and find the answers to your questions and concerns?

He Is Both Willing and Able to Heal

Let's talk about a common dilemma that many Christians struggle with today. You believe that Jesus is able to heal but wrestle with doubt as to whether or not He is willing to heal you. Until you discover the answer to this question you will not be able to stand firm in the faith and accept your healing.

In Luke 5:12, there is a man who asks Jesus the same question. *"And it happened when He was in a certain city, that behold, a man who was full of leprosy saw Jesus; and he fell on his face and implored Him, saying, 'Lord, if You are willing, You can make me clean.'"* He knows Jesus can heal, but he's not sure if He is willing to heal him.

Jesus responds to this man in verse 13, *"Then He put out His hand and touched him, saying, 'I am willing; be cleansed.' Immediately the leprosy left him."* Just as Jesus is willing to heal this man of leprosy, He is willing to heal you too.

JESUS USES A HOLISTIC APPROACH TO HEALING

Jesus is concerned about our complete system—spirit, soul, and body. He uses a very holistic approach to insure that we are healed and made whole. He believes in holism. He knows when we are disjointed that we are in pain.

He does not simply put a Band-Aid over a weepy, infected wound. He takes the time to carefully clean out the infection from the wound first and then sutures it shut by the stripes of His whipping.

> *Now may the God of peace Himself sanctify you completely; and may your whole spirit, soul, and body be preserved blameless at the coming of our Lord Jesus Christ* (1 Thessalonians 5:23).

He doesn't just heal the heart, He checks around that heart to find the root of the problem.

HEALING THE WHOLE PERSON

The whole person is spirit, soul, and body. The spirit is the eternal being who will either spend eternity in heaven or hell. This is our decision alone to make. God does not desire to send anyone to hell. We send ourselves there if we reject Jesus Christ as our Savior. John 3:16 says, *"For God so loved the world, that He gave His only begotten Son, that whoever believes in Him shall not perish, but have eternal life"* (NASB). The first step to becoming whole is to surrender to Jesus.

The soul is the second part of our being, and it includes the mind and the emotions. Oftentimes the physical body is sick because the soul needs healing. The ungodliness of today's society, the selfishness of others, and even our own bad decisions cause great injury to this part of our being. God shares His desire for us in Jeremiah 30:17: *"For I will restore health to you and heal you of your wounds."* Emotional wounds and physical healing go hand in hand with one another. By God's grace we can learn how to forgive, let go of the past, move forward, and allow the soul to heal.

The third part of our being is the physical body. This is the part that we see every day; it houses our spirit and soul, and God appoints it a time to be born and a time to die (see Eccles. 3:2). But even though it is temporal, Jesus received severe whippings so that it too can be healed and made whole (see Isa. 53:4-5).

God cares about the whole person—spirit, soul, and body. So much so that He records a prayer for its well-being in Third John 1:2: *"Beloved, I pray that you may prosper in all things and be in health, just as your soul prospers."*

DOES GOD WITHHOLD HEALING?

You hear that healing is the bread of God's children. So, you pray, you wait, and then you start to wonder, "Does God withhold healing?" To answer this question we need to go to God's healing Word.

From there He arose and went to the region of Tyre and Sidon. And He entered a house and wanted no one to know it, but He could not be hidden. For a woman whose young daughter had an unclean spirit heard about Him, and she came and fell at His feet. The woman was a Greek, a Syro-Phoenician by birth, and she kept asking Him to cast the demon out of her daughter. But Jesus said to her, "Let the children be filled first, for it is not good to take the children's bread and throw it to the little dogs." And she answered and said to Him, "Yes, Lord, yet even the little dogs under the table eat from the children's crumbs." Then He said to her, "For this saying go your way; the demon has gone out of your daughter." And when she had come to her house, she found the demon gone out, and her daughter lying on the bed (Mark 7:24–30).

This seems like a harsh response from Jesus toward this Gentile woman who asked Him to heal her daughter from demon possession. But you see, this event took place under the old law; Jesus had not yet shed His blood for our redemption. And salvation had not yet come to the Gentiles either. This woman did not have covenant rights under the Jewish law.

But her response to Jesus is amazingly faith-filled. *"Yes, Lord, yet even the little dogs under the table eat from the children's crumbs."* She's not calling upon the letter of the law, which she has no right to, but upon the mercy, the unmerited favor of the Lord. And she receives what she humbly requests, and her daughter is set free from demon possession.

Since this time, the atonement for sin and the consequences of sin, such as sickness and disease, have been paid in full by the redemptive blood of Jesus Christ (see Chapter 2). According to Romans 11:11–36, salvation has come to the Gentiles, and they have been grafted into the blessing. We no longer have to beg for healing like this Gentile woman did.

The blessing of healing has already been bestowed upon us: *"by His stripes we are healed"* (Isa. 53:5), and again in First Peter 2:24, *"who Himself bore our sins in His own body on the tree, that we, having died to sins, might live for righteousness—by whose stripes you were healed."*

So in response to this question, "Does God withhold healing?" the answer is no. In my spirit I hear, "The Bread and the Wine have already been served."

It isn't that God is withholding healing. Jesus already broke bread (His body) for us when He bowed down and gave His back to be brutally whipped for our healing. He also poured the wine (His blood) when He shed His blood at Calvary, so that we can live under a new covenant—a blood covenant called grace. The grace given to us is that we share freely in the blessing of healing because Jesus worked it out with the Father on His own back.

PARTAKE OF THE BREAD OF LIFE AND BE HEALED

Jesus is the bread of life that was broken and given to us so we can be healed. Jesus says of Himself in John 6:35, *"I am the bread of life. He who comes to Me shall never hunger, and he who believes in Me shall never thirst."* This is why we can say that healing is our bread. We who believe have covenant right with the Father by the blood of Christ to be healed. Jesus asks us not to forget what He did for us by partaking of a supernatural meal with Him called Communion.

> *For I received from the Lord that which I also delivered to you: that the Lord Jesus on the same night in which He was betrayed took bread; and when He had given thanks, He broke it and said, "Take, eat; this is My body which is broken for you; do this in remembrance of Me." In the same manner He also took the cup after supper, saying, "This cup is the new covenant in My blood. This do, as often as you drink it, in remembrance of Me." For as often as you eat this bread and drink this cup, you proclaim the Lord's death till He comes* (1 Corinthians 11:23–26).

Some of God's people take communion every morning before they start their day, remembering what the Lord did for them and accepting all of His benefits He so graciously provided for them. Others take it as the Spirit quickens them in their home, surrounded by family and friends, again giving thanks for the blood covenant they have with the Father and blessing the Lord Jesus Christ for redeeming them from the curse. Many others partake of the Lord's Supper with their local place of worship, reminding themselves of the sufferings of Christ and all that He provided for them.

However we partake of the Lord's Supper, we are to be careful that we do not take it in an unworthy manner. Let's read:

> *Therefore whoever eats this bread or drinks this cup of the Lord in an unworthy manner will be guilty of the body and blood of the Lord. But let a man examine himself, and so let him eat of the bread and drink of the cup. For he who eats and drinks in an unworthy manner eats and drinks judgment to himself, not discerning the Lord's body. For this reason many are weak and sick among you, and many sleep. For if we would judge ourselves, we would not be judged. But when we are judged, we are chastened by the Lord, that we may not be condemned with the world* (1 Corinthians 11:27-32).

WARNING: You are not to partake of the Lord's Supper in an unworthy manner. In other words, if you are not born again, meaning you have not first believed in your heart that Jesus is the one and only way to salvation, and then confessed this aloud with your mouth, you are not to partake of communion. If you do, you will be guilty of the body and the blood of Jesus.

Also, you are to examine your own heart; if there is sin, deal with it. Confess it and rid yourself of it. If you do not first examine yourself and partake in communion, you bring judgement upon yourself. You curse yourself, and this is one reason that many are weak and sick and spiritually asleep among your fellowship. Never should the Lord's Supper be taken lightly.

DON'T BLAME GOD, SEARCH YOURSELF

When healing is not manifesting, I have learned to stop blaming God and to start searching within myself to find out what is happening in my life that is hindering the healing power of God.

Why does it appear that I am getting worse and not better? If I don't know the answer, I ask the Holy Spirit to show me what's in my heart. I can do this without feeling condemned because I know that His grace is for me and not against me. He willingly gives the revelation so that I can be healed.

Take the time to examine your heart and ask yourself the following questions:

- Am I struggling with past hurts and unforgiveness? Matthew 6:14-15 tells us, *"For if you forgive men their trespasses, your heavenly Father will also forgive you. But if you do not forgive men their trespasses, neither will your Father forgive your trespasses."*

- Is there willful sin in my life? Psalm 66:18 makes it plain, *"If I regard iniquity in my heart, the Lord will not hear."*

- Am I speaking the blessings of God or the curses of satan over my life? Proverbs 18:21 teaches us that, *"Death and life are in the power of the tongue, and those who love it will eat its fruit."*

- Have I surrendered my five senses and human reasoning over to God? Or do I trust them more than the Word of God concerning my healing? We can learn from our spiritual father, Abraham, in Romans 4:19, *"And not being weak in faith, he did not consider his own body, already dead (since he was about a hundred years old), and the deadness of Sarah's womb."*

- Are my eyes fixed on Jesus? Or have I lost my focus and they are centered on the illness? Hebrews 12:2 tells us where our eyes should be focusing, *"looking unto Jesus, the author and finisher of our faith."*

- Have I given in to confusion and doubt? Am I being controlled by a spirit of fear? Or am I walking by faith? Second Timothy 1:7 says, *"For God has not given us a spirit of fear, but of power and of love and of a sound mind."*

- Do I really believe that God is for me and not against me? Romans 8:31 says, *"What then shall we say to these things? If God is for us, who can be against us?"*

If the Spirit of God is speaking to your heart, stop what you are doing, start praying and seeking God for His forgiveness and guidance, and start the healing process again.

HE RESTORES HEALTH TO ME

God has provided us with spiritual means to restore health and to keep us healthy in the long run.

What's the secret? God's people continue their quest to obtain long life and good health with diet, exercise, and supplements, and still many continue to fall ill and die prematurely. Even though these are wise choices, they are not enough. What's the secret to restoring our health?

God reveals this secret in Proverbs 4:20–22. He says, *"My son, pay attention to my words and be willing to learn; open your ears to my sayings. Do not let them escape from your sight; keep them in the center of your heart. For they are life to those who find them, and healing and health to all their flesh"* (AMP).

We need to remember that we are spiritual beings who live inside physical bodies. If we do not attend to our spiritual needs, we will wear out and become weak emotionally and physically.

So how do we attend to our spiritual needs? First of all, did you notice that He says, "My son"? He is referring to a spiritual family member. If you aren't a member yet, this is the first step to living a healthy life. Then He instructs us to attend to His words. We are to listen and do what the Word says to do. He tells us to submit to His sayings, which means we are to yield or surrender to the will or authority and power of the Word of God. Last but not least, He tells us to not allow biblical teachings to depart from our sight. We are to live life entwined with His teachings.

All these other things that we do like eating better, exercising, and taking supplements are good, but they do not take the place of God's Word and promise to us. If we attend to our spiritual needs according to His ways, then He promises *healing and health to all our flesh.*

HE HEALS ME OF MY WOUNDS

As a healing evangelist, I meet many people with many needs, and for whatever reason certain individuals stand out in my memory. One such individual was a young man I met in the healing line. He was newly born again and struggling with addictions to alcohol, drugs, pornography, and other sexual sins. Remember, he was fresh out of the world. His state of being is understandable, and the good news with him is that he was seeking godly help to be free from unrighteousness and healing for his wounds.

When he received Jesus as his Savior, he was instantly born again. *"Therefore, if anyone is in Christ, he is a new creation; old things have passed away; behold, all things have become new"* (2 Cor. 5:17). Even though this spiritual experience is an instant miracle, making Jesus the Lord of your life is not; it is progressive.

It has to deal with our willingness to overcome the desires of the flesh and tame the human will. Even more challenging than this is getting to the root of the problem. This is when we need to be open and honest with one another and allow Jesus to anoint us with the balm of Gilead.

What about all those who call themselves followers of Jesus who are drowning in their sins, and they do not care? They are so sinful they no longer recognize right from wrong.

In the Book of Jeremiah 8:22, the prophet, himself weeps for his people and cries out, *"Is there no balm in Gilead, is there no physician there? Why then is there no recovery for the health of the daughter of my people?"*

Why was Jeremiah so distraught? The people were so spiritually sick. They were bound by iniquities, perversities, sins of false teachings, perpetual backsliding; they held fast to deceit; they heard but would not listen; they refused to repent; they did not heed the judgment of the Lord; they rejected the word of the Lord; they were given to covetousness; from the prophet even to the priest everyone dealt falsely; and they were not ashamed of the abominations they committed (see Jer. 8). This portion of Scripture could very well be an update on the state of the local church today. She needs the healing balm of Gilead.

You may be wondering, what is the balm of Gilead? A balm is an aromatic, medicinal substance derived from plants. Gilead was an area east of the Jordan River well-known for its spices and ointments. The "balm of Gilead" was, therefore, a high-quality ointment with healing properties. The balm was made from resin taken from a flowering plant in the Middle East, although the exact species is unknown. It was also called the "balsam of Mecca." Myrrh is taken from a similar plant—*Commiphora myrrha*. The Bible uses the term *balm of Gilead* metaphorically as an example of something with healing or soothing powers.[1] It comes from the Hebrew word *tsĕriy* and it means to crack (as by pressure), hence, to leak (Strong's, H6875). The name *Gilead* itself means a "rocky region" (Strong's, H1568)

We have been given the healing balm of Gilead—His name is Jesus Christ. He is the only medicinal salve that can redeem His people, but they have to be willing to repent of their sins, make Jesus Christ their Lord again, and surrender to the supernatural healing power of the Holy Spirit. He will heal them first spiritually, by the power of repentance, then heal their mind and emotions, by the transforming power of the Word of God. They must learn to believe and readily receive the supernatural *sōzō* power to heal and make us whole again in Jesus' name.

Couple Healed of MS and Parkinson's Disease

It was the last teaching session at a recent healing seminar in Harrisonburg, Virginia when an elderly couple made their entrance into the church building. The husband was in a wheelchair suffering from Parkinson's disease. His wife who was faithfully pushing the wheelchair was also suffering, but from MS.

It did not appear to me that she knew anyone in the meeting, but she said that the Lord told her that she was to bring her husband to this meeting.

Now, I want to bring you up to speed here—this is the same healing seminar where Betty was healed from Parkinson's disease about two or three months earlier. We read about her at the end of Chapter 3, where she shares her testimony.

It's now time to administer the healing power of the Holy Spirit to the people. The woman wheels her husband to the front. My faith perks up as I hear the woman tell us what ails the man—Parkinson's disease. All of us present in this meeting know that we know this is no coincidence, but a divine appointment ordered of the Lord. And it was.

I, along with Betty and the others, lay healing hands upon the man. I ask the people to pray in the Spirit. I renounce the spirit of premature death, Parkinson's disease, a paralytic spirit, and nerve damage. I command the man to be loosed, to be free to walk again, his bodily functions to return, and memory loss to be healed along with other things as well.

I encourage the man to put his faith into action and start to move his feet, ankles, knees, and legs. He cooperates with the move of the Holy Spirit, and slowly but surely he begins to loosen up. After a short while, I ask him to go for a walk with Jesus.

A few of the men help him out of his wheelchair, and begin to walk him around. At first his feet slide forward because his knees aren't completely loose yet. But as he keeps taking strides forward we can all witness his knees straightening out. They continue to walk him around and around in circles as he gets stronger and stronger. His precious wife stands there with tears in her eyes as she witnesses her husband's body come back to life.

Then, as the men continue to walk with the man, we ask her if she has a need for healing. Well, she says that in fact she does have a physical need. She struggles with MS. So we ladies circle around her, put our faith into action, and the physical symptoms start to leave her body one by one. The joy and the tears flow from everyone present in that place.

Our Lord Jesus Christ is not only able but so willing to heal us spiritually, emotionally, and physically too. Let us partake of the Bread of Life, drink from the cup of the new covenant, believe for our health to be restored, and allow Him to lavishly anoint us with His healing balm of Gilead to heal our wounds.

PRAYER

Dearest Jesus,

I did not understand until now that You truly are both able and willing to heal and make me whole again in spirit, in soul, and in my body.

Forgive me because I was ignorant and thought You withheld healing from me, but in reality I have a part to play to activate Your sōzō power.

I see how intricate Your healing procedure is. It's more than putting a Band-Aid over an infected wound. You desire to go in and supernaturally scrape away the spiritual infection first and then fill us with your healing balm of Gilead and, when we are ready, suture it closed by the stripes of Your whipping.

I partake of the Bread of Life and drink from the cup of Your new covenant to restore my health and to heal me from all wounds.

In Jesus' name, I pray, amen.

Do you identify Jesus Christ as your Jehovah Rapha, your Great Physician? Do you realize that He has a medical report for you? Turn to the next chapter and find out what this report says.

✝

SELF-EXAMINATION

Am I grateful for the healing power of Jesus Christ? Do I believe that He is both willing and able to heal and make me whole again? Do I still believe God withholds healing from me? Or am I ready to face the fact that the conflict is with me, not with God? Do I partake of the Lord's Supper unworthily? Or am I in right standing with Him? Do I need my health to be restored? Am I ready to have Him rub His salve on me, the healing balm of Gilead?

NOTE

1. "What Is the Balm of Gilead?" GotQuestions.org, accessed May 16, 2016, http://www.gotquestions.org/balm-of-Gilead.html.

CHAPTER 8

✝

THE GREAT PHYSICIAN

"Jehovah Rapha is my great physician. His medical report declares that His spirit gives life to my mortal body, and my faith makes me whole."

What's in a name? Plenty. In my readings of the Bible, I see destiny is often attached to someone's name. The same is certainly true of God's name here, *Jehovah Rapha*. Jesus Christ fulfilled His name in Isaiah 53:5, *"by His stripes we are healed."*

Jehovah is translated as "The Existing One" or "Lord." The chief meaning of *Jehovah* is derived from the Hebrew word *havah* meaning "to be" or "to exist." It also suggests "to become" or specifically "to become known." This denotes a God who reveals Himself unceasingly. *Rapha* (*râpâ'*) means "to restore," "to heal," or "to make healthful" in Hebrew. When the two words are combined—*Jehovah Rapha*—it can be translated as "Jehovah Who Heals." (see Jer. 3:22; 30:17; Isa. 30:26; 61:1; Ps. 103:3). *Jehovah* is the Great Physician who heals the physical and emotional needs of His people.[1]

In Exodus 15:26 it says, *"For I am the Lord who heals you."* Jesus Christ is Jehovah Rapha, the Lord who heals. He understands the pathology of all sickness and disease. More importantly, this great physician knows the cause of illness, has the remedy, and is the cure for all sickness and disease. The ultimate pathway to healing flows through His veins. Healing is in the blood of Christ.

What other doctor is there who has His credentials? Doctor Jesus created the human body. He understands it inside and out. He possesses the revelation of every cell, tissue, organ, and system within it. He designed it and orchestrated it to function together in harmony to produce life, and life in abundance.

How often have we heard someone say that they have to do whatever the doctor tells them to do? Even when they have been told they will die within a short matter of time and there isn't anything they can humanly do for them. But they recommend them to continue to take the same medication or treatment that obviously does not work for them. There are times when we humans make no sense! This is one of those times.

I am going to speak forthrightly with you. It is a religious spirit amongst Christians that rises up against the healing power of Jesus Christ. A religious spirit is not something you want to hold on to. It is an antichrist spirit that proudly resists Him and His ways, but the good news is that you do not have to stay bound to this spirit. You can get free by repentance and stay free by studying the Bible and believing and doing what it says. Trust me when I say Doctor Jesus wants you to be free from this wicked spirit, and He wants to heal you too.

His Report Declares

God's Word makes remarkable claims for us to be healed. To the unregenerated soul, mind, and emotions His promises can sound too good to be true. This is why we are to transform our unbelieving minds by the unadulterated Word of God. *"And do not be conformed to this world, but be transformed by the renewing of your mind, that you may prove what is that good and acceptable and perfect will of God"* (Rom. 12:2). Health and healing are in the perfect will of God.

The Word of God cleanses the body of Christ (see Eph. 5:26). It cleanses us from sin, including doubt and unbelief. We can boldly come to the throne of grace that we may obtain mercy and find grace to help in time of need (see Heb. 4:16). If your need is healing, then you need to study the Word concerning healing.

LIFE TO MY MORTAL BODY

The Great Physician, Jehovah Rapha, has not abandoned you on some deserted island without a means of defense. He has given you supernatural power to overcome the wiles of the enemy. This power comes from His Spirit, the Holy Spirit. According to Romans 8:11, *"But if the Spirit of Him who raised Jesus from the dead dwells in you, He who raised Christ from the dead will also give life to your mortal bodies through His Spirit who dwells in you."* He has given you resurrection power.

Let me ask you, "Is there deadness in your body somewhere?" Take a moment and ponder upon the supernatural power you have been given to resurrect dead body parts.

One woman suffered from throat cancer, and she underwent radiation treatments to stop this wicked disease. But the radiation treatments destroyed her saliva glands and made swallowing miserable. She was given medication to help her produce saliva, but it was not working well.

Several years had already passed when she heard about a healing service in her area. She attended and heard a message of hope and healing. As healing hands touched her, the same supernatural power that raised Christ from the dead was released and instantly those dead saliva glands were resurrected and produced saliva on their own.

Right off the top of my head, I can think of three women who were no longer able to produce natural tears. But by the release of the resurrection power of the Holy Spirit all three received their healing instantly and no longer need special eye drops.

Countless numbers of people who had deaf ears now hear.

115

Many women who had barren wombs are now able to bear healthy children.

Do you hear what God has given to you? You do not have to settle for dead body parts. Believe and receive all that He has for you.

FAITH

Along with His Spirit, He gives to us the spiritual weapon of faith to overcome every attack of the enemy, including sickness and disease. Let's examine faith.

Faith is a spiritual power that we inherit from God to use in our everyday life to access divine intervention for a healing or a miracle. God Himself operated in the realm of faith in Genesis 1 when He created the heavens and the earth. Because He creates people in His image, He grants us the right of passageway into His supernatural realm of the miraculous by our faith in Him.

Hebrews 11:1 tells us, *"Now faith is the substance of things hoped for, the evidence of things not seen."* Faith is not abstract; it's not about emotions or feelings. It says faith is a substance, an actual foundation upon which we stand. As I share with you in Chapter 1, faith has a precursor—hope.

In this work, I believe I stir hope within you for healing. By the time you finish this book you can say that you are more than ready to access what you have need of from the Lord by your own faith.

WHERE IS YOUR FAITH?

The disciples were sailing across Lake Gennesaret with Jesus:

> *But as they sailed He fell asleep. And a windstorm came down on the lake, and they were filling with water, and were in jeopardy. And they came to Him and awoke Him, saying, "Master, Master, we are perishing!" Then He arose and rebuked the wind and the raging of the water. And they ceased, and there was a calm* (Luke 8:23-24).

Then He asks them a pertinent question: "Where is your faith?"

Perhaps you are like the disciples here—you are sailing along in life when out of nowhere a life-threatening storm hits. Waves of negative reports surround you and say you are in jeopardy. You cry out to Jesus, "I am perishing!" and Jesus responds to you, like He does to the disciples, "Where is your faith?"

Now, most would take this response as a rebuke, and yes, it is. But why not assess His response from different point of view?

You have a choice to make—you can either place your trust in the strength of the storm to overtake you, or you can place your confidence in His strength to overcome this life-threatening storm raging against you.

WHY DID YOU DOUBT?

Now in the fourth watch of the night Jesus went to them, walking on the sea. And when the disciples saw Him walking on the sea, they were troubled, saying, "It is a ghost!" And they cried out for fear. But immediately Jesus spoke to them, saying, "Be of good cheer! It is I; do not be afraid." And Peter answered Him and said, "Lord, if it is You, command me to come to You on the water." So He said, "Come." And when Peter had come down out of the boat, he walked on the water to go to Jesus. But when he saw that the wind was boisterous, he was afraid; and beginning to sink he cried out, saying, "Lord, save me! And immediately Jesus stretched out His hand and caught him, and said to him, "O you of little faith, why did you doubt?" And when they got into the boat, the wind ceased (Matthew 14:25–32).

Through the centuries, Peter receives a lot of gruff for sinking halfway from the boat to Jesus, but even so Jesus meets Him where he is and pulls him up again.

Maybe you're like Peter? You hear Jesus call out to you to step out of the boat, walk on the water, and meet Him. You obey, but halfway to the manifestation of your miracle you lose your focal point. It can happen to anyone. You start to focus on the wind and the waves raging around you, and you start to sink.

If this is you, don't let discouragement get the best of you. Just like Jesus does with Peter, He extends His hand of salvation—grab hold of it. Let Him pull you up again and continue to walk on the water.

I told you before and I will say it again, but in a different way. When you step out of the boat and walk in faith for your healing, satan will come after you like a mighty raging storm. He will try to get your focus off of your Healer, Jesus, and back on the storm of the disease. But Jesus remains your lifeguard, and when you call out to Him He will come to you. When you see His hand, seize it. He will lift you up so you can continue on your faith walk of healing.

YOUR FAITH MAKES YOU WHOLE

When we consider faith for salvation, we need to remind ourselves the meaning goes beyond that of eternal life in Heaven. Remember the teaching in Chapter 3—the meaning of the word *save* or *saved* comes from the Greek word *sōzō* and means to save, deliver, protect, heal, preserve, do well, and be made whole.

When we actuate our faith, it brings about God's great saving grace for the need we have in any given situation. The point is that it is our faith in Christ that makes us whole.

Jesus responds to the woman with the issue of blood found in Luke 8:48, *"Daughter, be of good cheer; your faith has made you well. Go in peace."* To the one leper who returns to give thanks for his healing Jesus says in Luke 17:19, *"Arise, go your way. Your faith has made you well."* Again, we see in Luke 18:42 Jesus admonishes the blind beggar, *"Receive your sight; your faith has made you well."*

These are three different examples where Jesus speaks to the receiver that it is their faith that heals and makes them whole. Why is this important to note? Because oftentimes God's people wait for Him to do the miraculous, while He waits for us to cultivate our faith to believe for our healing. For the believer in Jesus, it is our faith in His healing power that brings forth health, healing, wholeness.

Let's move on to another important topic to help stimulate your faith to go to God for your healing.

GOD LISTENS AND DELIVERS

How often do you hear people complain that their doctor doesn't have the time to listen to them?

Your Great Physician actually listens when you call to Him (see Ps. 4:3). But do you know that there is a certain type of prayer that draws His attention to us? This type of prayer is filled with words of faith. In Mark 11:24 Jesus gives us instruction about how to pray, *"Therefore I say to you, whatever things you ask when you pray, believe that you receive them, and you will have them."*

Not only does He listen, but according to Psalm 34:17, *"The righteous cry out, and the Lord hears, and delivers them out of all their troubles."*

There are many different troubles that come with sickness and disease, especially when the world labels it long term. One trouble is financial. The woman with the issue of blood who bled for 12 years, whom we mentioned above, spent all her livelihood on physicians and could not be healed by any (see Luke 8:43).

The thief not only steals our health and life with sickness and disease, but he will also use the illness to dry up our finances so we are like the woman above and we have no resources to seek further help. This causes people to feel desperate and without hope.

FREE HEALTH CARE

As God's people, we are never without hope. God is on our side and has prepaid our spiritual medical bills.

His healing service to us is free, but that does not mean it's cheap. He provides it to us at a very high price to Him. This prepayment is His shed blood as He endured unimaginable suffering for us and because of us at Calvary.

Even though we do not pay for His healing power, we do have to be proactive with our faith and believe to initiate His healing power.

HEALING IS A GOOD GIFT

Some Christians really squawk when they hear someone teach or testify about healing, as if healing were an evil thing. They would be less convicted for their doubt and unbelief if the person were not healed to begin with. But we are not going to be like the squawkers. Instead, we are going to ponder on the goodness of this gift of healing. *"Every good gift and every perfect gift is from above, and comes down from the Father of lights, with whom there is no variation or shadow of turning"* (James 1:17).

Healing is a gift from God, and is found throughout the Bible. In other words, healing is biblical. Because it comes from our Savior Himself, it is beyond good—it's great!

For those suffering from severe pain, God's gift of supernatural healing is the greatest pain reliever there is. When a man suffering from a seven-year migraine receives supernatural healing and all pain instantly disappears, he starts to rejoice. When a woman's painful and crippled arthritic hands heal, she sheds tears of joy.

Does the mama of a ten-year-old girl, who was born with a deformed hip that never grew correctly and caused her little girl daily pain and suffering, question if healing is good or evil? Of course not; she knows by the witness of her own heart and by the smile on her daughter's face that this is only good, and she glorifies God for His healing power.

When these people receive their healing, they do not question if healing is evil. No, they know it's good, and they know it comes from God. It changes their life, and they can't help but testify of His goodness to others.

God's gift of supernatural healing is good and perfect.

HIS MEDICAL POLICY NEVER CHANGES

There is an unrest inside of God's people with the ever-changing medical policies today. But in God's medical center that never happens. His policy never changes. Why? Remember what it says in Hebrews 13:8? *"Jesus Christ is the same yesterday, today, and forever."* And concerning the Word of the Lord, it declares in First Peter 1:24-25, *"All flesh is as grass, and all the glory of man as the flower of the grass. The grass withers, and its flower falls away, but the word of the Lord endures forever."*

God and His Word are steadfast. You can always count on Him. The Lord says in Jeremiah 1:12 in the Amplified Version of the Bible, *"I am [actively] watching over My word to fulfill it."* Even if the world changes, He does not. When people within the body of Christ fall away, He remains faithful. There is everlasting security in this fact—His medical policy never changes.

> *Surely He has borne our griefs and carried our sorrows; yet we esteemed Him stricken, smitten by God, and afflicted. But He was wounded for our transgressions, He was bruised for our iniquities; the chastisement for our peace was upon Him, and by His stripes we are healed* (Isaiah 53:4-5).

God's best is always divine healing. He's the Creator of the human body. He's the Great Physician; with Him there is never a hopeless situation. His diagnosis is always correct. Instead of repairing or replacing with artificial parts, He recreates a new part for you. There's no risk of infection or rejecting new body parts. His work is perfect. There's no haggling with insurance companies because it has all been covered by His blood, and for you the price is just right—it's free.

AM I TOO LATE TO BE HEALED?

Maybe you are concerned that the hour is too late for you to be healed? If this is what you think, think again.

Jesus stands before His dear friend Lazarus' tomb and requests they roll away the stone, but Martha, Lazarus' sister, reasons with Him, *"Lord, by this time there is a stench, for he has been dead four days"* (John 11:39). But Jesus does not heed Martha's doubt; instead He calls out in faith to the dead body:

> *"Lazarus, come forth!" And he who had died came out bound hand and foot with graveclothes, and his face was wrapped with a cloth. Jesus said to them, "Loose him, and let him go"* (John 11:43–44).

No matter how late in the game you think it is, He can still heal. I know what I speak of—our son was raised from the dead (see Chapter 9 for more details.)

Abraham by faith received strength to father a child.

> *(As it is written, "I have made you a father of many nations") in the presence of Him whom he believed—God, who gives life to the dead and calls those things which do not exist as though they did; who, contrary to hope, in hope believed, so that he became the father of many nations, according to what was spoken, "So shall your descendants be." And not being weak in faith, he did not consider his own body, already dead (since he was about a hundred years old), and the deadness of Sarah's womb. He did not waver at the promise of God through unbelief, but was strengthened in faith, giving glory to God* (Romans 4:17–20).

> *By faith Sarah herself also received strength to conceive seed, and she bore a child when she was past the age, because she judged Him faithful who had promised* (Hebrews 11:11).

In fact, according to Genesis 17:17 she was 90 years old.

Just considering the healings and miracles that took place in the lives of these three people, I encourage you and say, "No, it is not too late for you to be healed in Jesus' name."

HE MAKES HOUSE CALLS

What a blessing, the Physician of all physicians still makes house calls. In Luke 4:38-39, Peter's mother-in-law is sick with a high fever, and he asks Jesus to heal her. Jesus stands over her and rebukes the fever, and she heals instantly, rises from her bed, and serves them.

In Luke 8:40–56, we read how Jairus falls down at the feet of Jesus and implores Him to come to His home and heal his daughter who is on her deathbed. Jesus agrees, but the young girl dies before they arrive. Jesus is not discouraged by the news and encourages Jairus not to be afraid but to believe and she will be healed. When they arrive they are met by the mourners and the scoffers, but Jesus remains strong in the faith. He does not allow any doubters to enter into the room where the dead body lies. He only enters in with Peter, James, and John and the girl's parents and tells the little girl to arise, and she comes back to life.

I witness some of the greatest miracles during private house calls, and you can too. Study the faith lessons of Jesus, and put your faith into action.

WHAT DO YOU WANT ME TO DO FOR YOU?

In Luke 18:41, Jesus stops on the side of the road and asks the blind beggar man who is calling out to Him, *"What do you want Me to do for you?"* A couple thousand years later, the Great Physician is asking you the same question.

Obviously, this blind beggar was not poor in faith. From the riches of his faith, he confidently responds, *"Lord, that I may receive my sight!"*

What's your response to the Great Physician?

RICH FAITH VERSUS POOR FAITH

With the healing testimony above from the Book of Luke, we see that the blind beggar was not poor in his faith but rich. At first, he sat on the side of the road and begged Jesus to have mercy on him. But as soon as he engaged in conversation with Jesus, he stopped the begging. When Jesus asked what he wanted Jesus to do for him, he answered with surety, *"Lord, that I may receive my sight!"*

Spiritually speaking, what is the financial condition of your faith? Are you rich or poor in faith? If you are poor in your faith, you need to work for a while and make some deposits in your faith bank until your faith is rich and you believe for your healing, just like the blind beggar did. If your faith is rich, it's time to trust Jesus and receive your healing.

AMY'S RICH FAITH MAKES HER WHOLE

We tend to make the things of God so complicated that it is difficult for people to believe. It doesn't have to be this way, and in all honesty it shouldn't be. When we mature in our faith, we will return to the sweet surrender of the childlike faith that He desires from us. We will believe and do what He says because our faith is rich and we naturally trust Him.

Think of a newborn baby—when he or she is hungry, they do not stop to question whether or not Mama has milk; they just receive what they have need of. We need to trust the Lord this way, richly.

Being in the healing ministry, I take in the most profound workings of faith by observing children. They are not bound up with unbelief; they are free to trust and receive. Let's learn to believe for the miraculous from the example of this little girl.

There was a little girl in our elementary school named Amy who struggled to read. No matter how hard she tried she was unable to read. One night she felt especially discouraged. Her parents spoke with her and encouraged her to pray to God and ask Him for help.

Later during the night, the parents felt concern and decided to go to her room to pray with her, but they were amazed at what they found. Their daughter was already on her knees beside her bed praying to Jesus, asking Him from the richness of her faith to help her to read.

The Bible says in Hebrews 4:16 that we are to *"draw near with confidence to the throne of grace, so that we may receive mercy and find grace to help in time of need"* (NASB). We are to go boldly before the throne of grace and make our needs known. There are two faith steps that we need to take into account in order to go boldly before His throne of grace and receive.

1. We need to learn to trust Him richly. *"Fear not, for I am with you; be not dismayed, for I am your God. I will strengthen you, yes, I will help you, I will uphold you with My righteous right hand"* (Isa. 41:10).

2. In order to trust Him we need to know Him as the God who cares. *"Casting all your cares [all your anxieties, all your worries, and all your concerns, once and for all] on Him, for He cares about you [with deepest affection, and watches over you very carefully]"* (1 Pet. 5:7 AMP).

It's after we have taken these two faith steps that we can go boldly before His throne of grace like this little girl did and receive. And what did she receive?

The next morning, Amy woke up with anticipation, ran with excitement to tell her parents that she could now read, and began to read to them aloud.

Learn to trust in Jehovah Rapha, the Great Physician, like Amy did and activate your faith richly in Him so you can be made whole.

PRAYER

Dear Jehovah Rapha,

You are my Great Physician, the Lord who heals me. There is no other like You. You understand the pathology of all sickness and disease, and more importantly, You know the cause of illness. You have the remedy; You are the cure for all sickness and disease.

You created my body. You possess the revelation of every cell, tissue, organ, and system within it. You designed it and orchestrated it to function together in harmony to produce life, and life in abundance.

Your medical report declares that health and healing are in Your perfect will and that they are good gifts given to us for our benefit.

Your Spirit gives life to my mortal body, and no matter how bad the situation looks, it is not too late for my body to heal.

I exercise my faith richly in Your healing word and I am made whole.

In Jesus' name I pray, amen.

Turn to the following chapter and learn about a personal choice that you must make in a life and death situation and how to activate a couple of God's supernatural medicines.

✝

SELF-EXAMINATION

Have I gained a greater understanding of Jehovah Rapha, my Great Physician? Do I recognize His supremacy over the human body and why He knows how to heal it? Do I struggle with His medical report that says His Spirit gives life to my mortal body? Do I have sick and weak body parts that need to be resurrected or healed? Do I have a clearer understanding about faith? Do I have rich faith or poor faith? How do I strengthen it? How do I activate it? Do I understand that it is my faith in Him that makes me whole? Do I see now it's not too late for me to be healed? Am I willing to make a house call and minister healing to those who are in need?

NOTE

1. Chris Poblete, "The Names of God: Jehovah Rapha," The BLB Blog, July 27, 2012, http://blogs.blueletterbible.org/blb/2012/07/27/the-names-of-god-jehovah-rapha.

CHAPTER 9

✝

CHOOSE LIFE, LAUGHTER, AND JOY

*"I accept His advice to choose life that I may live. I
receive beauty for ashes, the oil of joy for mourning,
the garment of praise for the spirit of heaviness. I take
His medicine—laughter and joy for my strength."*

Are you at a crossroads in life? Is life difficult today? Does the mountain appear too big to climb? Is there a struggle on the inside of you to make the right choice? And of utmost importance, will your decision glorify God and bless others?

Everything you do today will involve a decision that you need to make. Will your decision be right or wrong?

The Bible gives us the best advice in decision making. It says to choose Jesus, choose the straight and narrow path, choose to serve the Lord, choose the good fight of faith, choose to believe, choose to love, choose to give, choose to forgive, to name just a few. Today He says, "Choose life."

CHOOSE LIFE

Regardless of the crisis we face, God gives us the best option, and that is to choose life. Deuteronomy 30:19 declares, *"I call heaven and earth as witnesses today against you, that I have set before you life and death, blessing and cursing; therefore choose life, that both you and your descendants may live."*

We should also realize that our decisions today will impact our future generations. If we desire to walk in the blessings of God, then our choices need to be godly ones. Wrong choices will result in negative consequences, not only for us but for our descendants as well.

Abortion

We live in a day and an age when society devalues human life, especially the life of the unborn child. I understand the issues that are involved, but nonetheless everyone has the godly right to life. Regardless of their stage of development while in the womb, predicted physical conditions or limitations, or the situations in which they were conceived, I still believe in the biblical principle that all people are created in the mirror image of God. As unpopular as my beliefs may be, I stand firm in my convictions and I am pro-life. I choose life.

There are many excuses today why women think they should abort their children. Not one of these reasons will ever alter my stance on the value of human life.

Some say, *"The mother is too young, or she is just a child herself."* I recently met a dear lady who shared with me her life story. She showed me a photo of her as a very young teenage girl holding her three-week-old baby girl before giving her up for adoption. I had tears in my eyes as she shared with me in detail how difficult it was to give her up for adoption. But years later, she has been reunited with her adult daughter. Hurts have been healed as they have come to know and understand one another. The cycle of their family was not cut off by abortion, but through adoption their family grew.

Young unwed mothers are told, *"Your parents will be angry when they find out."* They probably will be, but their anger does not override that baby's right to life. Perhaps this young unwed mother's child might be the one God chooses to discover a cure for a disease that is plaguing our society. Or will marry and give birth to a child who eventually does discover a cure. Whatever their future holds, God has a plan for them, and the baby has the right to live and fulfill his or her destiny.

I lived through this experience when I was 18 years old, pregnant and unmarried. With encouragement and Christian discipleship, my boyfriend and I married, and we have been married for 35-plus years. Being young and not feeling adequate to be a mother I prayed to God a simple but heartfelt prayer, *"God, please teach me to be a good mom."* He honored that prayer. Today, my husband and I have three grown biological children, five adopted boys, seven grandchildren, and a children's home in Guatemala for abandoned children, orphans, and children born with HIV. I have become a spiritual mother to many people around the world.

Being young, pregnant, and unmarried does not have to be the end of a good future. If you give the situation over to God, it is just the beginning with a rough start. Our Lord Jesus is willing and able to see you through. He is faithful and can be trusted.

Angry voices cry out, *"What about rape victims who find themselves pregnant?"* I agree with you that rape is an unacceptable crime, but punish the one who is responsible, the rapist, not the innocent child. Women all around the world have suffered rape; some aborted their babies while others gave their babies the greatest gift of all, unconditional love, and put their children up for adoptions or chose to keep and raise their babies themselves.

Other women, married or not, say to themselves and to others, *"I am not ready for a child. I have my career to pursue."* This is certainly not a reason to end the life of a child. If you honestly do not want your child, then give your child to someone else who does. Adoption preserves the life of your child, your dignity, and gives the opportunity for your child to fulfill their destiny as well.

We have five adopted sons; the youngest is Marcos. He survived several abortion attempts. A Christian nurse intervened before the last attempt at a hospital and gave a plan of hope to the birth mother—instead of abortion, put the baby up for adoption. We received Marcos when he was one day old. He later died at one month old from SIDS (Sudden Infant Death Syndrome). But by the true power of faith, we raised our son from the dead, and believed and received by faith a new heart, new lungs, new kidneys, and a new brain. With God all things are possible! You can read his miraculous testimony in my first work, *Dare to Believe*.

What happens when the pregnant mother receives a terrible medical report about the unborn child? With today's technology this happens, but there is a real God who offers hope to the hopeless.

I had the opportunity to minister healing to two unborn children this past year. Both mothers were told to abort their children because of health issues concerning their unborn babies. Both were Christians and said no they would not do that. By faith in our Lord Jesus Christ, both children were healed while in the womb and were born healthy and whole.

> *Now to Him who is able to do exceedingly abundantly above all that we ask or think, according to the power that works in us, to Him be glory in the church by Christ Jesus to all generations, forever and ever. Amen* (Ephesians 3:20-21).

You say, *"I know of families whose children were born with physical challenges."* I do too, and the beauty of these families again is the unconditional love that is given to these children and the love that these children give to their families.

I was born with physical challenges, but my relatives pitched in and helped my parents through the difficult times.

What it all boils down to is that society devalues human life because they deny God and the biblical teachings that reveal the true value of people and the plans and purposes that He has for us.

If you find yourself in this situation today, He is encouraging you to choose life today.

Suicide and Assisted Suicide

We are going to turn to another serious subject right now and speak very candidly about suicide and assisted suicide. This is a painful matter to discuss, but we must.

There are also famous verses found in Ecclesiastes 3:1-2, *"To everything there is a season, a time for every purpose under heaven: a time to be born, and a time to die; a time to plant, and a time to pluck what is planted."* God has destined when we will be born and when we will die. In Deuteronomy 30:19, He instructs us to choose life.

No matter what people may say, what message the media will try to portray, or what excuse satan will whisper in your ear, you never take your own life or assist someone else to end their life.

Yes, satan is the one who will tell you to end your life. He will use other people to convince you that there is no hope, especially in this day and age when human life is devalued. These things are wrong, they are evil in the sight of God, and they come from the pit of hell.

As followers of Christ, we need to be proactive and teach people that they are valuable, that there is a reason for them to live.

The Bible tells us in John 10:10 that the thief, satan, comes to steal, to kill, and to destroy. Let me ask you, what do suicide and assisted suicide do? They steal, kill, and destroy, and satan is the author of this evil.

Jesus continues to say in the same verse, *"I have come that they may have life, and that they may have it more abundantly."* You may think that your life is not worth living. Perhaps your body is racked with sickness and disease. Jesus includes you in His plan of atonement. He offers you life and life in abundance through the supernatural gift of healing and deliverance.

According to God's standards, you never end your own life, nor do you assist someone else to take their life. These are demonic-guided activities.

God says choose life today.

Never Give Up

Are you in the midst of a raging battle? Do you feel like it's time to give up?

We all face battles in this life, but some are more difficult than others. After time, one can be tempted to give up the fight and let the enemy win. Don't!

God has given you everything you need to win this battle. You have fought long and hard to get this far and have done everything you know to do. Even still, the enemy is unrelenting. What do you do now?

After having done everything, we are encouraged in Ephesians 6:13 *to stand*. That's right, *stand*. Don't sit down and give in to the enemy, but *stand strong*. Dig in our heels, be unmovable, fight the enemy to the finish, and never give up.

> *Therefore take up the whole armor of God, that you may be able to withstand in the evil day, and having done all, to stand* (Ephesians 6:13).

God's Thoughts About You

One major reason people lay their spiritual armor down, give up, and die is because they feel God doesn't love them and that He doesn't care about their struggle. This is why we as followers of Christ need to be take the initiative and tell them and show them just how much He really does care for them and love them.

Perhaps the person in this battle is you, and you are the one who needs to be encouraged to not give up today. Did you know that God thinks about you? Does this give peace or cause a twinge of fear? When you understand what the Bible says it will bring you peace and comfort.

Psalm 139:17-18 reveals the types of thoughts He thinks concerning you. It says, *"How precious also are thy thoughts unto me, O God! How great is the sum of them! If I should count them, they are more in number than the sand: when I awake, I am still with thee"* (KJV).

According to this scripture, the Lord has more than just a few good thoughts about you. In fact, you cannot count the total sum of them.

We live in such a negative world that people have a difficult time sharing a pleasant thought about another. But despite the negativeness of this world, God can't stop thinking good thoughts about us.

His thoughts about us are more than good thoughts, they are precious thoughts. When something is precious, it is valuable, priceless, beyond the limit of a price tag. When something is precious, it is important, significant, and it matters. When something is precious, it is treasured, very dear to the heart. When something is precious, it is cherished, esteemed very highly. And we are the somethings that are precious and loved, appreciated, respected, esteemed, treasured, cherished, prized, and held very dear to His heart.

When He thinks about us, He thinks to Himself how valuable and important we are to Him, how much He treasures us and cherishes us, and how precious we are to Him.

His thoughts are this way because His love for us is unconditional. We cannot earn His love by doing good works. His love for us is given freely. Nor can we lose His love by bad behavior either.

Did you know that God does not have bad children? He does have children that have done bad things, that's called sin. And what did He say to those that wanted to stone the woman that was caught in the act of adultery? *"He who is without sin cast the first stone."* And one by one her accusers walked away. And what did He say to this woman? *"Your sins are forgiven, go and sin no more."* He could not do this if His thoughts towards her were wicked.

Roman 5:8 comforts us with these words, *"But God commendeth His love toward us, in that, while we were yet sinners, Christ died for us"* (KJV).

His love for us is unconditional. There are no requirements to be met in order to be loved by Him. In fact, whether we love Him or not, He still loves us. He is for us and not against us. John 3:16 says, *"For God so loved the world, that he gave his only begotten Son, that whosoever believeth in him should not perish, but have everlasting life"* (KJV). God loves us so much that He gave His best, His Son, Jesus Christ to redeem us. He couldn't do this if He thought we were not worth redeeming.

Jesus Christ loved us so much that He willingly shed His blood on the Cross to save us from our sins, to heal us of all sickness and diseases, to set us free from all bondages. And He promises to make us whole. Jeremiah 31:3 assures us, *"Yea, I have loved thee with an everlasting love: therefore with lovingkindness have I drawn thee"* (KJV). In order to redeem us His thoughts had to be pure and wholesome about us.

He loves us unconditionally, and thinks *only* the best about us.

God has supernatural medicines that heal us in our spirit, soul, and body. We are going to discuss two of these here—laughter and joy.

LAUGHTER

For many of God's children, laughter is not a laughing matter. His people are so weighted down by the hurts of this world they forget how to laugh, let alone smile. Many are on antidepressant drugs or other substances because they simply want freedom from the pain in their life.

I believe that by the power of the Holy Spirit we can start to laugh again, even when life hurts. Why? Because laughter is more than a response to a witty joke or a funny story. It's one of God's supernatural medicines with actual healing properties within each laugh.

Ecclesiastes 3:4 tells us that there is *"A time to weep, and a time to laugh; a time to mourn, and a time to dance."* Yes, there is a time to weep and a time to mourn, but this is a period of time, not a perpetual state of being. God so wants to heal your mind and your emotions so that you can laugh and even dance again.

Beauty for Ashes

Maybe your heart is so broken that you don't even know where to begin to pick up the pieces, but your heavenly Father knows how:

To console those who mourn in Zion, to give them beauty for ashes, the oil of joy for mourning, the garment of praise for the spirit of heaviness; that they may be called trees of righteousness, the planting of the Lord, that He may be glorified (Isaiah 61:3).

What does it mean *beauty for ashes?* During times of great sorrow, the mourner would sit down in the ash pit and cover themselves with the ashes to demonstrate the deep pain and hurt they felt.[1]

The word *beauty* comes from the Hebrew word *pě'er* and is a head-dress, ornament, or turban (Strong's, H6287). This message from Isaiah conveys how the Messiah ministers to our deepest inner wounds—by removing our turban of ashes filled with mourning and sadness, and in exchange He adorns us with His supernatural joy and beauty.

The Oil of Joy for Mourning

The oil of joy for morning, or the anointing of the Spirit in lieu of that plenteousness of tears which naturally belonged to mourners,[2] is a super-natural inner healing anointing from the Holy Spirit for God's children to apply during their time of mourning.

I remember many years ago, I met a sweet-tempered woman who had lost all five of her children in one night during a horrific accident. I was a complete stranger to her, but she opened up to me; for whatever reason, she felt I was a safe person for her to share her deepest hurt in life and the journey she went through to heal.

This inner healing doesn't mean she forgets her children or that they are no longer an important part of her life. What it does mean is that in His great mercy for her, He goes into the secret crevices of her soul, her mind, and her emotions, and carefully brings her back into the stream of life where she feels safe to open her heart again to others and truly smile, laugh, and even dance again. What He does for this woman He will do for you.

Now, when I met this woman she had a sweet temperament about her, but as she shared that is not the way she was before her healing.

Unfortunately, after the death of her children she turned to alcohol, but it couldn't take away the pain. It just compounded this deep pain in life. She blamed God, others, and even herself for the tragedy. She became an angry alcoholic and very dysfunctional.

Before we finish with her testimony, we need to set the record straight on something.

Did God Take Her Children?

To set the record straight we need to look at this tragedy through the eyes of God's Word. Did God take her children? According to John 10:10, it is the thief, satan, who comes to steal, to kill, and to destroy—not God. Continuing on in this passage, Jesus tells us that He came to give us life and life in abundance. So let me ask you again, "Did God take her children?" No, He did not; satan did.

But you say, "He allowed it!" What He allows to every person is a free will. The freedom to make choices, both big and small. Sometimes we make wrong decisions, and even a seemingly harmless one can cause grave consequences. So am I saying it's the fault of humans? Sometimes yes and sometimes no. Quite frankly, putting the blame for a tragedy on God or on a person doesn't bring healing. What does bring healing is the truth.

What is the truth in these matters? John 16:33 tells us that "*in the world you will have tribulation*," meaning in this world we will pass through difficult times, not because God has ordained it but because we have an enemy, satan, who is bent upon our destruction.

If you blame anyone, then you need to blame satan. He is the one responsible. Jesus is your helper in time of need.

Apply the Oil of Joy

Despite her anger, bitterness, and alcoholism, she had a few friends who remained faithfully at her side. Somewhere along the line, her friends had found the greatest healer of all, Jesus Christ. They shared Him with her, and she accepted Him as her Savior and made Him her Lord.

He went into those deep, dark crevices of her soul, and He shed the light of His healing Word and brought her back to the place called "life" where she was again able to smile, laugh, love, function, and even dance again. This did not happen overnight; it was a process. He continued to heal the woundedness of her soul as she allowed Him entrance.

I want to give you these words sung by David in Psalm 30:11, *"You have turned for me my mourning into dancing; You have put off my sackcloth and clothed me with gladness."*

The Garment of Praise

There is a supernatural garment He gives to us that causes us to step into the realm of victory. It is called praise. We see throughout the Bible that God's people praise their way through seemingly impossible situations.

For you this seemingly impossible situation may be an unexpected pregnancy, the loss of someone you love dearly, enslavement to addiction, or sickness and disease. Whatever the situation might be, praise will lift you out of the pit of despair.

When we praise God during the storms of life, our focus shifts from the uncertainty in the storm to the greatness of our God to see us through. Hope arises, worry lifts off of us, clarity of mind comes forth, and negative emotions lose their power when we praise the Lord.

The Benefits of Laughter

As I mentioned above, laughter possesses healing properties. It relieves stress and pain and aids in the healing process in other ways. Let's look at the list of short-term and long-term benefits of laughter compiled by the Mayo Clinic.

A good sense of humor can't cure all ailments, but data are mounting about the positive things laughter can do.

Short-Term Benefits

A good laugh has great short-term effects. When you start to laugh, it doesn't just lighten your load mentally, it actually induces physical changes in your body. Laughter can:

- Stimulate many organs. Laughter enhances your intake of oxygen-rich air; stimulates your heart, lungs, and muscles; and increases the endorphins that are released by your brain.

- Activate and relieve your stress response. A rollicking laugh fires up and then cools down your stress response and increases your heart rate and blood pressure. The result? A good, relaxed feeling.

- Soothe tension. Laughter can also stimulate circulation and aid muscle relaxation, both of which help reduce some of the physical symptoms of stress.

Long-Term Effects

Laughter isn't just a quick pick-me-up, though. It's also good for you over the long haul. Laughter may:

- Improve your immune system. Negative thoughts manifest into chemical reactions that can affect your body by bringing more stress into your system and decreasing your immunity. In contrast, positive thoughts actually release neuropeptides that help fight stress and potentially more serious illnesses.

- Relieve pain. Laughter may ease pain by causing the body to produce its own natural painkillers. Laughter may also break the pain-spasm cycle common to some muscle disorders.

- Increase personal satisfaction. Laughter can make it easier to cope with difficult situations. It also helps you connect with other people.

- Improve your mood. Many people experience depression, sometimes due to chronic illnesses. Laughter can help lessen your depression and anxiety and make you feel happier.[3]

There Is Strength in Laughter

Almost always after a healing service, the Holy Spirit will cause me to laugh so hard I feel like I am going to bust. Interestingly, He doesn't cause me to laugh this way publicly, but privately. By the time I am done laughing I am energized and strengthened. My mind has settled down and is ready to sleep.

Take Your Supernatural Medicine

Illness steals your laughter, weakens your strength, and hinders your healing. It can easily become a vicious cycle of depression, pain, and more sickness. So whether or not you feel up to a good laugh, you need to make a decision and just do it—laugh.

You might feel phony at first, and that's okay. Look at it in this way—you need to take your medicine. With practice you will find that it is easy to laugh with the Lord. I believe before you know it He will cause you to laugh when you need it most, and your spirit, soul, and body will be full of strength.

Healing and Miracles Restore Laughter

Sarai could not envision herself ever having a child. She, like Abram, her husband, had no hope, and instead of seeing God as her hope she blamed Him for her barrenness. Assessing the situation at hand, applying everything but faith, she came up with a plan. Abram agreed and conceived a child with her maidservant, Hagar (see Gen. 16). This plan was not God's plan; it was conceived of the flesh, not by faith, and it gave no glory to God. Sarai too had a hard lesson to learn, for now she was despised in the eyes of her maidservant.

When the Lord changed Abram's name to Abraham, He also gave Sarai a new name. She was now Sarah, declaring that she would bear a son, and she would be a mother of nations; kings of peoples would come from her womb that once was barren. God loves to bring forth the possible from the impossible. It reveals His mighty hand and leads many people to Him.

Like Abraham, Sarah had a decision to make in this miracle as well. When she first heard the prophetic message from God's messengers that she would bear a child, she laughed with doubt and unbelief. When the messengers of the Lord asked why she laughed, she lied and denied that she had laughed, but they corrected her. God knows what's in our hearts, and our hearts need to be rid of all doubt and unbelief in order to conceive a miracle.

Most of us remember that Sarah laughed at the prophetic word spoken by God's messengers, but Abraham laughed too with doubt and unbelief (see Gen. 17:17–19). He actually fell on his face and laughed! He started to reason in his heart once again about their ages; he was now 100 years old and Sarah was 90 years old. Sarah was past childbearing years. Those were the facts, but do the facts limit God's power?

Abraham actually was bidding with God that He would bring the blessing through his son, Ishmael. God said no; He wouldn't do that. He was going to bring about His promise to Abraham by the way of faith and not according to the flesh.

In response to Abraham's human reasoning, God said to him, *"Is anything too hard for the Lord? At the appointed time I will return to you, according to the time of life, and Sarah shall have a son"* (Gen. 18:14). Abraham made the decision to trust God. This time he did not take into account his age or his aged body, the lack of his physical strength, or that Sarah was an elderly barren woman. Instead, he focused on the greatness of his God.

Sarah too lined herself up with the promise of God that she would bear Abraham's son in her old age. God's promise did come to pass, just as He said it would. She conceived a child at the age of 90 by her own faith, and that barren womb supernaturally opened up and she bore a son.

> *By faith Sarah herself also received strength to conceive seed, and she bore a child when she was past the age, because she judged Him faithful who had promised* (Hebrews 11:11).

He took away her shame and sorrow and gave her a baby son named Isaac. Isaac means "laughter." Her laughter of doubt and unbelief that she had been called on earlier was transformed by His supernatural power. God had not forgotten her; her joy was restored through this miracle.

JOY

Nehemiah 8:10 tells us that the joy of the Lord is our strength. Joy is often thought of as an emotion, but in reality is much more than a mere emotion. It is a supernatural strength given to us by God to empower us.

The Joy of My Salvation

Do you remember the joy of your salvation? I will never forget the day I received Jesus as my Savior. People who knew me before that glorious day would comment about how I just shone, and they wanted to know why. It was that evident.

I knew why—I found joy when I found Jesus, and I couldn't help but smile and laugh. *"Yet I will rejoice in the Lord, I will joy in the God of my salvation"* (Hab. 3:18). And why wouldn't I rejoice about my salvation? It is the best thing that has ever happened in my life.

This joy of our salvation is contagious. When we are genuine in our faith, people want what we have. It is meant to be shared with others. There is even great rejoicing in Heaven over our salvation. *"Likewise, I say to you, there is joy in the presence of the angels of God over one sinner who repents"* (Luke 15:10).

Finding the Fullness of Joy

> *You will show me the path of life; in Your presence is fullness of joy; at Your right hand are pleasures forevermore* (Psalm 16:11).

There are two gateways to choose from in this life—the narrow gate or the wide gate. Only one of these gates leads to His presence where there is the fullness of joy. Matthew describes these two gateways for us:

Enter by the narrow gate; for wide is the gate and broad is the way that leads to destruction, and there are many who go in by it. Because narrow is the gate and difficult is the way which leads to life, and there are few who find it (Matthew 7:13-14).

Contrary to society's beliefs, the wide gate isn't all that it is cracked up to be. It can only bring temporary satisfaction because sin is only pleasurable for a season (see Heb. 11:25). In the beginning sin is pleasurable, but this wears off quickly. It leaves the sinner feeling letdown and empty, searching for more, and it leads to eternal death.

God's gateway is the one that is straight and narrow, and it leads to the blessing of being satisfied, fulfilled in His presence.

Activate His Fullness of Joy

Okay, we find Jesus, and at the same time we discover our joy. But how do we obtain the fullness of His joy? The baptism of the Holy Spirit will enhance His power in us. He will rev it up to full and overflowing like we desire.

First of all, you have to be willing to receive the power of the Holy Spirit. It says in Acts 1:8, *"But you shall receive power when the Holy Spirit has come upon you."* He will eagerly come upon you with His power if you will receive of Him.

You activate the fullness of His joy for edification when you pray in the Spirit, or in tongues. *"He who speaks in a tongue edifies himself"* (1 Cor. 14:4).

If you will believe in the Lord Jesus Christ and receive of this power, John 7:38 says this will happen, *"He who believes in Me, as the Scripture has said, out of his heart will flow rivers of living water."*

The Holy Spirit can intervene and help us when we are baptized in the Holy Spirit with the evidence of speaking in our heavenly supernatural language:

Likewise the Spirit also helps in our weaknesses. For we do not know what we should pray for as we ought, but the Spirit

Himself makes intercession for us with groanings which cannot be uttered (Romans 8:26).

This empowerment of the Holy Spirit is for the born-again believer and to the generations that follow them.

Then Peter said to them, "Repent, and let every one of you be baptized in the name of Jesus Christ for the remission of sins; and you shall receive the gift of the Holy Spirit. For the promise is to you and to your children, and to all who are afar off, as many as the Lord our God will call" (Acts 2:38-39).

We activate the fullness of joy when we are in His presence, and we obtain the measure of fullness when we are baptized in the Holy Spirit and pray in tongues.

Joy Poppers

A joy popper is anyone or anything that steals your joy. For example, I will not watch sad movies of people dying from cancer; no, I need to build my faith in the Word and believe for it to be healed in Jesus' name. Below is a short list of things that can rob your joy.

* Anger

* Feuding with one another

* Unforgiveness

* Self-pity

* A negative word, conversation, or report

* Sad and depressing movies, stories, or articles

* Sickness and disease, especially long-term illness

* The premature death of a loved one

* Pain

* Sin

Depression Busters

Take responsibility for the state of your well-being and do whatever you can do to break free from depression. Here is a short list of depression busters that God has provided for you to help you get free and stay that way.

* Give your life to Jesus and become born again.

* Press into God's presence.

* Activate the baptism of the Holy Spirit.

* Rekindle the joy of your salvation.

* Encourage yourself as you pray in the Holy Spirit.

* Get healed from sickness and disease.

* Forgive those who have done you wrong and move forward.

* Stop rehearsing your failures.

* Read or listen to a message of hope found in God's Word.

* Put on the garment of praise.

* Sing and dance and make a joyful noise.

* Put a smile on your face.

* Laugh at the enemy.

* Choose your friends wisely; hang out with positive people.

Healed From TMJ and Smiling Again

Illness steals a person's joy and their desire to smile and laugh, as was the case with Bridgete Cash from Buena Vista, Virginia.

About two years ago, Bridgete heard about a healing service that was going to be held in a nearby church in Lexington. The Holy Spirit prompted her that she needed to go to this meeting. She arrived from work just as the meeting was about to start, so she sat near the back of the church. After the message, the altar was opened up for people who needed to have hands laid upon them for healing. Now, let's read what Bridgete has to say as the altar call was given.

> I thought to myself, that's me. I had suffered for five years from TMJ (Temporomandibular Joint Disorder). And nothing could be done. I was eating eight Ibuprofen a day, and Tylenol in between, and still was having breakthrough pain. I would lay in bed at night and just cry and rub my face because it would hurt so much.
>
> Having no relief from pain medications, I also went to physical therapy and acupuncture. But nothing provided any relief!
>
> I was at the point where I didn't even want to smile because I didn't feel good. I couldn't smile because it hurt my face. I didn't want to eat because everything just hurt. My life had taken a complete downturn.

In case you do not know, here is a medical explanation of what Bridgete says she is suffering from. The temporomandibular joint acts like a sliding hinge connecting the jawbone to the skull. Temporomandibular Joint Disorder can cause pain in the jaw joint and in the muscles that control jaw movement.[4]

Bridgete continues to tell us what happened as she was about to be healed.

> So, I went up and Becky laid her hands on me, and I could just feel it. I went and sat down in a chair and I thought to myself, I do feel different, something is different on the inside of me. By the next morning the pain had completely gone. I have not had one pain since then from TMJ. I was completely healed, through her touch by the Lord. And I thank God every day.

God's supernatural healing power delivers us from sorrow and pain and restores our laughter and joy so we can smile again.

And the ransomed of the Lord shall return, and come to Zion with singing, with everlasting joy on their heads. They shall obtain joy and gladness, and sorrow and sighing shall flee away (Isaiah 35:10).

PRAYER

Dear Heavenly Father,

Even if life is difficult for me today, I accept Your advice—I do not give up, but I choose life. If someone else is in a rough spot this day, I will speak to them and let them know that their life counts. I will be proactive with my faith and let people know that we are all precious and valuable to You.

I take the responsibility for my emotional and physical well-being, I receive Your beauty for my ashes, the oil of joy for mourning, I put on the garment of praise for the spirit of heaviness, and I choose to grab hold of Your supernatural medicines, laughter and joy. To regain my physical strength I put a smile on my face and I start to laugh again. I rekindle the joy of my salvation, and I press into Your presence so that my joy may be full. I activate the power of the Holy Spirit, pray in tongues, and encourage my spirit in You.

I will keep a sharp eye out for joy poppers and not allow negative people or ungodly activity to rob me of my joy. I will do whatever is necessary to break free from depression and activate all the depression busters that You have provided for me.

In Your name, dear Jesus, I pray, amen.

Turn to the next chapter and discover the healing power of repentance and forgiveness and learn how to heal.

✝

Self-Examination

Do I have tough decisions to make today? Am I willing to accept God's advice and choose life in every situation, knowing this decision will affect future generations? Do I struggle with depression? Is there a deep hurt that I need to pray with someone about? Can I honestly say I am able to smile and laugh? Do I need to go over the checklist of joy poppers and make some adjustments in my life? Am I applying everything on the depression buster list so I can be free from all depression?

Notes

1. Andrew Robert Fausset, "Biblical Definition of Ashes," Bible History Online, accessed May 18, 2016, http://www.bible-history .com/faussets/A/Ashes.

2. "Isaiah 61," Pulpit Commentary, accessed May 18, 2016, http:// biblehub.com/commentaries/pulpit/isaiah/61.htm.

3. Mayo Clinic Staff, "Stress Relief from Laughter? It's No Joke," Mayo Clinic, April 21, 2016, http://www.mayoclinic .org/healthy-lifestyle/stress-management/in-depth/stress-relief/ art-20044456.

4. Mayo Clinic Staff, "TMJ Disorders," Mayo Clinic, December 13, 2012, http://www.mayoclinic.org/diseases-conditions/tmj/basics/ definition/CON-20043566.

✝

CHAPTER 10

THE HEALING POWER OF REPENTANCE AND FORGIVENESS

"I heed His counsel and repent, rid myself from bitterness, forgive others, and empower my faith by love."

The Spirit of God is reaching out to you with His message of healing. He is teaching you how to heal in spirit, in soul, and in body. Therefore, the question you should be asking yourself now is, "Am I willing to heed His counsel?"

Some of you, especially those who have a medical background, struggle with this message. It goes against everything you have been taught. I do not suggest that you toss all your knowledge aside but that you humble yourself before the sight of the Lord and realize that man's knowledge, even as advanced as it is, is no match against God's wisdom. His Spirit tells us:

> *"For My thoughts are not your thoughts, nor are your ways My ways," says the Lord. "For as the heavens are higher than the*

earth, so are My ways higher than your ways, and My thoughts than your thoughts" (Isaiah 55:8-9).

At a recent meeting, a beloved obstetrician in the community sat in the front row. After he heard how Jesus redeemed him from sickness and disease, he came forward to receive healing in his lower back. To his joy, his back was instantly healed. I then placed his hands in mine and placed them upon the next person in line. Interestingly, it was a pregnant woman who was in need of a miracle for her unborn child.

I encourage you within the medical field, with your medical knowledge and your understanding of the human body, not to limit the power of the Holy Spirit to heal but to align yourself with Him. Ask Him to reveal Himself strong to you. Before you tend to the next patient, ask the Lord what needs to be done in this person's situation and then pray with your patient. Activate your faith and heed His counsel to heal.

REPENTANCE HEALS

Sin is so prevalent within the body of Christ today. It slithers in slowly as believers keep quiet about what they observe around them. It is to the point now that many of God's people are full of deception, and they no longer recognize right from wrong. This sin is the cause of much sickness and disease today.

Let's look to the Book of Revelation for one probable cause for sickness in the Church today. Turn to your Bible and read Revelation 2:18–29, the message to the church in Thyatira. We can call this fellowship "the immoral church."

> *I know your works, love, service, faith, and your patience; and as for your works, the last are more than the first. Nevertheless I have a few things against you, because you allow that woman Jezebel, who calls herself a prophetess, to teach and seduce My servants to commit sexual immorality and eat things sacrificed to idols. And I gave her time to repent of her sexual immorality, and she did not repent. Indeed I will cast her into*

a sickbed, and those who commit adultery with her into great tribulation, unless they repent of their deeds. I will kill her children with death, and all the churches shall know that I am He who searches the minds and hearts. And I will give to each one of you according to your works (Revelation 2:19–23).

The church in Thyatira is the portion of God's people who refuse to repent of their immoral ways. They are so deceived that they even allow a spirit of Jezebel to lead them. Because they tolerate Jezebel in their midst they suffer with sickness and great tribulations or difficulties. Even their children are inflicted with pestilence.

I mentioned in Chapter 1 that as a healing minister, I have never seen God's people as sick as they are now. Along with the lack of teaching from the pulpits about supernatural healing, another reason for this is a direct consequence of allowing the evils of Jezebel to reign within the local fellowships.

The only way to free ourselves from the consequences of tolerating this wicked spirit is to repent because we did not take a stand against it and demand it to step down and leave. If the people do not want it to leave, then we must flee from its demonic control and immoral behavior. Then we ourselves must remain faithful to the teachings of Jesus Christ until the end of time or the Lord calls us home, whichever comes first.

PAGANISM IN THE CHURCH

Another probable cause for the rise of sickness in the Church today is the overt practice of New Age and any other pagan religion by the body of Christ. Let's take a closer look at one accursed activity that is widely accepted and heatedly defended by Christians today—yoga.

God's people bound by this Hindu practice will fight you tooth and nail to defend their claim that what they do is a Christian form of yoga. First of all, this is an oxymoron. Yoga is a Hindu expression of faith and not a Christian one. You cannot mix the two together and come out with Christian. No, you create compromise.

Second, let's discuss what they call *chakras*. Hindus believe there are seven chakras in the human body that run from the base of your spine to the top of your head. Supposedly these chakras are energy channels that correspond to different areas of the body and correlate to specific circumstances in your life. This is not Christian teaching. The Bible warns us in First Timothy 4:1, *"Now the Spirit expressly says that in latter times some will depart from the faith, giving heed to deceiving spirits and doctrines of demons."*

Third, the stretching exercises, which may seem innocent, are not. They are worship poses to the Hindu gods that you fashion with your own body. It doesn't matter if there is Christian music playing in the background and you are quoting Scriptures, you are still participating in a Hindu worship service and bowing to their false gods.

This act alone breaks the first and second commandments:

> *You shall have no other gods before Me. You shall not make for yourself a carved image—any likeness of anything that is in heaven above, or that is in the earth beneath, or that is in the water under the earth; you shall not bow down to them nor serve them. For I, the Lord your God, am a jealous God, visiting the iniquity of the fathers upon the children to the third and fourth generations of those who hate Me* (Exodus 20:3–5).

Fourth, the Hindu form of meditation is in direct opposition to the biblical form of meditation. The Hindu form is that you empty yourself, which in reality opens you up to demonic forces that enter into your soul, mind, and emotions and take root within your spirit, which brings a curse upon you, your physical body, and even upon your family. God's form of meditation can be found in Joshua 1:8. Let's read:

> *Keep this Book of the Law always on your lips; meditate on it day and night, so that you may be careful to do everything written in it. Then you will be prosperous and successful* (Joshua 1:8 NIV).

Last, the power of Om—even though it is a very simple sound, it is complex in meaning. Om is an ancient chant used in both Hinduism and Buddhism. Om is the whole universe melded into a single word, representing the union of mind, body, and spirit that is at the heart of yoga. Often chanted three times to keep the mind occupied while being trained to meditate at the start and finish of a yoga session.

You reply, "Well, I don't participate in that part." You're wrong; you do. Even if you remain silent during these chants, you still tolerate them. All words possess the power of life and death, including Om, and these chants are derived by Hindu and Buddhist witchcraft. They are working their evil in you. Paul asks us a pertinent question:

> *Do you not know that your body is the temple of the Holy Spirit who is in you, whom you have from God, and you are not your own? For you were bought at a price; therefore glorify God in your body and in your spirit, which are God's* (1 Corinthians 6:19-20).

Even if you change up the yoga session, you still compromise your faith and participate in Hinduism with your spirit, soul, and body. Jesus says in Matthew 22:37, *"You shall love the Lord your God with all your heart, with all your soul, and with all your mind."* He is referring to Elohim, Father, Son Jesus Christ, and Holy Spirit, not Hindu gods. Joshua petitions us to take a stand on whom we will serve:

> *And if it seems evil to you to serve the Lord, choose for yourselves this day whom you will serve, whether the gods which your fathers served that were on the other side of the River, or the gods of the Amorites, in whose land you dwell. But as for me and my house, we will serve the Lord* (Joshua 24:15).

This leads us to the exposure and warning to the church in Pergamum, or the "compromising church."

> *And to the angel of the church in Pergamos write, "These things says He who has the sharp two-edged sword: 'I know*

your works, and where you dwell, where Satan's throne is. And you hold fast to My name, and did not deny My faith even in the days in which Antipas was My faithful martyr, who was killed among you, where Satan dwells. But I have a few things against you, because you have there those who hold the doctrine of Balaam, who taught Balak to put a stumbling block before the children of Israel, to eat things sacrificed to idols, and to commit sexual immorality. Thus you also have those who hold the doctrine of the Nicolaitans, which thing I hate. Repent, or else I will come to you quickly and will fight against them with the sword of My mouth. He who has an ear, let him hear what the Spirit says to the churches. To him who overcomes I will give some of the hidden manna to eat. And I will give him a white stone, and on the stone a new name written which no one knows except him who receives it" (Revelation 2:12–17).

Again, the way to release yourself from this bondage of sin is to repent to the Lord for your involvement and then renounce the spirit of Hinduism and Buddhism, or any other pagan religion you are involved with, and turn away from it, never to return to it again.

Set Free from Yoga and the Physical Effects of It

Healing is part of God's plan of redemption and is found throughout the Bible. In these last days there are many counterfeit doctrines that promise healing, but they come with demonic attachments. As Christians we need to be extra careful what we align ourselves with.

Two Spirit-filled Christian ladies bought into the lie that yoga was harmless and in the right setting transformed into a Christian exercise class. After all, their Christian friends were doing it, so it must be alright. Wrong!

As Christians, we just can't do whatever others do. We have to judge it according to the Word. If we have to compromise the Word of God and make excuses to justify the activity, then it's not right.

Since their involvement, both these ladies suffered in the lower back and hip area, and neither were able to rid themselves of this constant pain.

We discussed the matter during a Bible study, and they both assessed the situation. They judged the practice of yoga with the Word of God. They admitted that their involvement with it was wrong, and they took the steps to freedom mentioned above. They asked the Lord to forgive them, and they renounced the demons that had latched on to them. Instantly they were both healed and have remained free from this pain.

Sexual Immorality

The sin of sexual immorality reigned in both the church in Pergamum and the church in Thyatira. It started at the top with the leadership. Either they were enslaved to sexual sins or they refused to address it from their pulpits and call it what it is—sin.

To the church of Pergamum, God says:

> But I have a few things against you, because you have there those who hold the doctrine of Balaam, who taught Balak to put a stumbling block before the children of Israel, to eat things sacrificed to idols, and to commit sexual immorality (Revelation 2:14).

Again, a similar rebuke is given to the church of Thyatira:

> Nevertheless I have a few things against you, because you allow that woman Jezebel, who calls herself a prophetess, to teach and seduce My servants to commit sexual immorality and eat things sacrificed to idols (Revelation 2:20).

These words *sexual immorality* come from the Greek word *porneuō*, which is translated into the English language as *pornography* (Strong's, G4203). Pornography is running rampant within the house of God. This is wrong.

Do you not know that the unrighteous will not inherit the kingdom of God? Do not be deceived. Neither fornicators, nor idolaters, nor adulterers, nor homosexuals, nor sodomites, nor thieves, nor covetous, nor drunkards, nor revilers, nor extortioners will inherit the kingdom of God (1 Corinthians 6:9-10).

As a healing evangelist, I minister healing to many people. Over and over again in the healing lines there are men, more men than I have ever seen before at the altar of God. This is a good thing, but I see something occurring that I cannot deny. It is all too frequent to push it aside.

Many of these men are suffering with hearing problems, either deafness in one or both ears or ringing in their ears, and they are having trouble getting healed. At the same time, they are weeping and confessing that they are addicted to pornography and they want out of this bondage. I'm telling you, this is so frequent that there is a spiritual connection.

When I lead them into a prayer of repentance first and then minister healing to their ears, they almost always receive their healing. Oftentimes, as soon as they repent from sexual immorality their ears are automatically opened.

In Revelation 2:17 and 29, both the church in Pergamum and the church in Thyatira receive the same word, *"He who has an ear, let him hear what the Spirit says to the churches."*

I believe the supernatural realm and the physical realm are interconnected. There is a spiritual connection between the physical ear and the spiritual ear. The message we tune into with our physical ear, the spiritual ear will receive. It will transmit the message directly into the spiritual heart or spirit; we then speak it out from our mouth and act it out in the flesh.

We are told that faith comes by hearing, and by hearing the word of God (see Rom. 10:17). Well then, the opposite is also true—doubt and unbelief increase by the refusal to hear God's Word.

God's Word is very clear that sexual immorality, including adultery and fornication, is sinful. Even if we look at one another with sexual lust, we commit adultery in our heart (see 1 Cor. 6:9-10; Matt. 5:27-28).

The Spirit of the Lord convicts the men that their involvement with pornography is sinful and they need to stop and repent now. But they refuse to listen and turn a deaf ear to Him. I believe this is why their physical ear is suffering from deafness or ringing from nerve damage. The physical and spiritual ear are connected.

When they open up their spiritual ears to the Lord and repent from this wickedness, their physical ears are healed.

CAN SIN AFFECT HEALING?

Can sin affect your healing? Absolutely.

> *But it shall come to pass, if you do not obey the voice of the Lord your God, to observe carefully all His commandments and His statutes which I command you today, that all these curses will come upon you and overtake you* (Deuteronomy 28:15).

Disobedience and sin are one and the same, and they open the door for satan to come to us and attack us with the curse of sickness and disease.

You need to examine your heart and be honest with yourself. Deal with the issue of sin. Then go to God with a sincere heart and ask the Father to forgive you. He will. He is faithful and just to forgive us from all unrighteousness, including sexual immorality (see 1 John 1:9). Get free from all sexual bondage because sin definitely hinders healing.

MONEY CANNOT ALWAYS PURCHASE HEALTH AND HEALING

Another reason God's people are so sick is the love of money—not that they have money, but that it has them.

Word is clear—you cannot love God and Mammon at the
. It is one or the other. Matthew 6:24 tells us, *"No one can
masters; for either he will hate the one and love the other, or
else he will be loyal to the one and despise the other. You cannot serve God
and mammon."*

Money cannot always buy health and healing, but God can. Actually, as we have studied in the Scriptures, He already purchased it for us by the blood of His Son, Jesus Christ. Jesus gave us His currency.

His currency is not based on earthly gold but backed by our Redeemer, Jesus. Therefore, it not limited by human knowledge and ability but has unlimited buying power because it is backed by the richest currency that has ever or will ever exist—the redemptive blood of Jesus.

So if you are serving mammon and earthly riches, you will enter into spiritual financial trouble. Because, as I stated earlier, it is limited in its purchasing power. It cannot pay for total health and healing. Its supply will run out.

According to Revelation 3, this group of believers does not recognize how poor and wretched they are.

> *I know your works, that you are neither cold nor hot. I could wish you were cold or hot. So then, because you are luke- warm, and neither cold nor hot, I will vomit you out of My mouth. Because you say, "I am rich, have become wealthy, and have need of nothing"—and do not know that you are wretched, miserable, poor, blind, and naked— I counsel you to buy from Me gold refined in the fire, that you may be rich; and white garments, that you may be clothed, that the shame of your nakedness may not be revealed; and anoint your eyes with eye salve, that you may see* (Revelation 3:15-18).

To be free from a spirit of mammon you need to renounce your servitude to it, repent to Jesus Christ for your self-centered pride and greed, and make Jesus your Lord.

FORGIVENESS

Every day we have opportunities to choose forgiveness. Spouses, children, friends, neighbors, colleagues, even complete strangers can hurt us. Therefore, we are faced with daily decisions to forgive, to ask for forgiveness, or to be bitter and full of vengeance.

Unforgiveness is a weapon of satan to destroy the offended person from the inside to the outside. If it is not dealt with it will turn into bitterness. The Bible says that bitterness dries up the bones (see Prov. 17:22). It dehydrates the flow of life from deep within the spirit, soul, and body.

The only way to be free from this is to choose the path of forgiveness. God's Word is very clear concerning forgiveness. It says in Matthew 6:14-15, *"For if you forgive men their trespasses, your heavenly Father will also forgive you. But if you do not forgive men their trespasses, neither will your Father forgive your trespasses."* You *must* choose forgiveness.

Three Steps to Forgiveness:

1. Ask the Father to forgive you for the offense you have done or for not being willing to forgive another person for what they have done to you.

2. Forgive yourself.

3. Ask the offended to forgive you.

RID YOURSELF OF BITTERNESS

Recently, I ministered over the phone to a woman who suffered from severe arthritis pain for many years. I asked her if she was angry and bitter toward someone, because the Bible says that bitterness dries up the bones. She immediately burst into tears and confessed that it was true. I explained to her the negative consequences of unforgiveness. The Bible says in Matthew 6:15 that if we do not forgive others then the Father cannot forgive us for our wrong doings. I went on to say that forgiveness is not based upon our feelings but is a quality decision of faith. It doesn't matter if we feel the other person deserves to be forgiven or not; God's Word says that we must forgive.

Matthew 16:15 says it this way in the Amplified Version of the Bible, *"But if you do not forgive others [nurturing your hurt and anger with the result that it interferes with your relationship with God], then your Father will not forgive your trespasses."*

Let's look to the Amplified Version of the Bible again to see how Proverbs 17:22 reads, *"A happy heart is good medicine and a joyful mind causes healing, but a broken spirit dries up the bones."*

I explained to her that when we walk in unforgiveness we bind ourselves with spiritual chains and it prevents the blessings of God, such as healing, from entering into our bodies.

I led her in a prayer of repentance and the weight of unforgiveness lifted off of her. She then received Jesus Christ as her Lord and Savior. I went one step further with her and ministered the baptism of the Holy Spirit to her, and she received and we rejoiced together in the Spirit.

I then exercised my authority over arthritis in the name of Jesus and the swelling and the pain started to lift off of her. I encouraged her to put her faith into action and do things that she could not do before. She started to bend her knees without pain; she then lifted her arms above her head and the arthritis pain in the shoulders disappeared.

Perhaps you are like this woman and struggle to forgive someone who has hurt you. I encourage you with this woman's testimony to make a quality decision and forgive by faith and release this person from your revenge. In doing so, you will loose your physical healing by activating the healing power of forgiveness.

JESUS CHOSE TO FORGIVE

Consider for a moment what the world did to Christ and what His physical body had to endure. He had been falsely accused, mocked and spit upon, abused, abandoned, crucified, and buried in a tomb. The situation appeared to be without hope.

The Servant's service was devalued, they twisted His message, the intentions of His heart were unjustly judged, they destroyed His reputation, and He was made out to be the evil one.

What did Jesus do? He stretched out His arms and cried out to the Father and said, *"Father, forgive them, for they do not know what they do"* (Luke 23:34).

The spiritual body of Christ is under attack today. What do we do? Get down on our knees and cry out to the Father, *"Forgive them, for they do not know what they do."* His forgiveness saves many, and our forgiveness opens the door for others to receive this same hope that we have been so graciously given.

Forgiveness is an outpouring of the love that Jesus Christ shed for us at Calvary.

LOVE EMPOWERS FAITH

One way to empower your faith is by love. There is no greater way. If you are low on love for someone, you are also low on faith. You can't allow your faith to run low on love. Tank up on love.

Everywhere we turn there is opportunity to take offense, especially right before a miracle manifests. The devil will make sure of it. Before you do, step back from the drama and pray for God's wisdom and grace on how you should handle the episode in a godly manner.

In the midst of a life-threatening disease, people feel worn down, their emotions run high, and all too often there is great feuding amongst family members. It's common to encounter them bickering, name calling, cursing one another, playing the blame game, and throwing temper tantrums and even objects at one another. You name it, the enemy has got them doing things they wouldn't normally do. He knows if he can get these people to walk in hate instead of love, he wins the battle and the loved one dies.

If you behave in an unloving manner, redeem the loss of time, apologize, and ask for forgiveness quickly. As I stated earlier, you cannot afford the consequence of this sort of behavior.

This type of atmosphere is not conducive for a miracle. Love creates the right atmosphere for faith to produce what we have need of, and in this case it is supernatural healing.

When you are tempted to hold on to a grudge or withdraw your love from someone who has deeply wounded you, pray to the Father. Ask Him for His love for this person. Maybe this person is a wayward spouse, a son, a daughter, your parent, or a sibling. Perhaps you have been betrayed by a dear friend, a business partner, or someone on the pastoral staff. Whoever it is and whatever they have done to you, walk in love and forgive.

Actually, when you do, the enemy loses his power over you. When you love someone who does not love you in return or does not act in a loving manner toward you, you empower your faith, and your miracle is that much closer.

When they complain against you, find a way to praise something that they do.

If they say they hate you, turn the other cheek and say, "Yes, I know, but I still love you."

If they say they wish you were dead, reply, "I'm so glad you are alive."

What you are doing is throwing a bucket of water on the fire of their anger, and it will stop. The demon in them will give up. *"A gentle tongue breaks a bone"* (Prov. 25:15). Then build yourselves up on your most holy faith, praying in the Holy Spirit (see Jude 1:20).

If you need to, get outside help for an intervention, and if this doesn't work ask them to leave until they can behave themselves. Whatever you do, do it in love and not out of vengeance. You must guard your heart from evil and empower your faith by love.

Watch Over Your Spiritual Heart

Are you aware that the condition of your spiritual heart affects your physical body? This is why God's Word gives instruction to *"Watch over your heart with all diligence, for from it flow the springs of life"* (Prov. 4:23 NASB).

In the natural, when the physical heart is sick the rest of the body suffers. The same is true with the condition of the spiritual heart, except that it controls every area of our being—spirit, soul, and body.

The spiritual heart is a vital organ and we need to diligently care for it. Here are two basic rules to maintain a healthy spiritual heart.

1. Love the Lord.

"And you shall love the Lord your God with all your heart, with all your soul, with all your mind, and with all your strength." This is the first commandment (Mark 12:30).

2. Love your neighbor as yourself.

And the second, like it, is this: "You shall love your neighbor as yourself." There is no other commandment greater than these (Mark 12:31).

When you are engaged in a battle for your healing or miracle, you must make sure to activate your love for God and for others. You cannot afford to fight against one another. It is absolutely necessary for you to deal with all unforgiveness and bitterness. God does not give you the spiritual right to be vengeful. He says that vengeance belongs to Him. Trust me when I say He knows how to handle the situation.

PRAYER

Dear Heavenly Father,

You are reaching out to me, teaching me by Your Holy Spirit how to heal in my spirit, soul, and body. I will heed Your counsel.

I repent from all sin that is attacking the body of Christ today. I will not tolerate the controlling spirit of Jezebel. I will not participate in pagan rituals such as yoga. I run from sexual immorality and into Your arms, dear Jesus. I renounce a spirit of Mammon. I confess I have not seen how wretched and poor I have become, but from this day forward You alone, Jesus, are

*my God, and I put all my trust in You. I will not turn a deaf
ear to Your sayings. I will do what You say and show me to do.*

*I rid myself of all bitterness. I forgive the people in my life who
have done me wrong, and in doing so I am forgiven.*

*I empower my faith by Your love. I love You with all my heart
and soul, and I love my neighbor as myself.*

In Jesus' name I pray, amen.

In the next chapter, we will discuss how to activate the Sword of the
Spirit to release your physical healing. Let's turn there now and stimulate
your healing.

✝

SELF-EXAMINATION

Do I recognize the hand of the Lord that desires to heal me? Am I
willing to heed His counsel and repent of the sins that are so prevalent
in the Church today? Am I struggling with any of the sins discussed in
this chapter? Am I free or am I bound by the control of Jezebel, pagan
practices such as yoga, sexual immorality, or the spirit of mammon? Do I
harbor bitterness in my heart toward someone? Am I willing to forgive so
that my own sins can be forgiven me? Do I love the Lord with all that is
within me? Do I love others as I love myself? In what areas do I need to
work on to heal?

✝

CHAPTER 11

THE SWORD OF THE SPIRIT

"With wisdom from on high I activate the Sword of the Spirit. With the realization that I possess the power of life and death in my tongue, I exercise His authority. I curse this sickness at its very root and seed and say no disease will prosper in my body. When I am weak I thank Him that He remains strong in me. I boldly declare His abundant life, healing power, and supernatural strength to overtake my body in Jesus' name."

As we reason together about healing, we conclude that our faith to heal is not based upon the logic of humans, the five senses, emotions, or physical abilities, but its foundation is upon the atoning works of Jesus Christ.

In our study we rely upon God's type of wisdom described in James 3:17, *"But the wisdom that is from above is first pure, then peaceable, gentle, willing to yield, full of mercy and good fruits, without partiality and without hypocrisy."* We concur throughout the teaching of this work that the Great Physician is both able and willing to heal us.

We now grasp the fact and believe that by His stripes we are healed and that we have been given the responsibility to activate His healing power in our lives. Without further ado, we take the next step and learn to use the Sword of the Spirit.

ACTIVATE THE SWORD OF THE SPIRIT

The Lord gives us an all-powerful supernatural weapon called the Sword of the Spirit or the Word of God. He gives us this sword to defend ourselves in the daily battles of life that rise up against us. The power of this supernatural sword is voice activated.

You also turn on the power for the Sword of the Spirit when you confess aloud the Healing Creed. As you do this, you unleash the atoning work of Jesus Christ over your spirit, your soul, or your mind and emotions and over your physical body and into its interior workings.

By the supernatural law of the spoken word of God, you speak life to your cells, tissues, organs, and systems of your body. You declare healing into your muscles, ligaments, tendons, nerves, joints, and bones. You activate creative miracles to non-existent body parts. You command resurrection power to the dead, whether they be dead organs—such as a dead heart, lungs, kidneys, or a dead brain—or dead people. You raise them up by the power of your spoken words in the name of Jesus.

The Sword of the Spirit cannot help us unless we first fill ourselves with it, do what it says, speak out words of faith, and live out those spoken words. Will you be a responsible warrior for Jesus Christ and take up your Sword of the Spirit and fight for life and healing?

LIFE AND DEATH ARE IN THE TONGUE

Do you realize that we—yes, you and I—possess the power of life and death in our tongues? With every word that comes from our mouths we either create or we destroy. We need to be careful to think before we speak, choose our words wisely, and release them with caution.

Meditate on this Scripture from Proverbs 18:21, *"Death and life are in the power of the tongue, and those who love it will eat its fruit."* A revelatory moment with the Lord about the message of this verse alone will radically change your life and bump you up a notch in the work of His kingdom business.

GUARD YOUR MOUTH

There is wisdom from on high throughout the Holy Bible about this supernatural law of the power of the spoken word. How about this Scripture verse in Proverbs 13:3, *"He who guards his mouth preserves his life, but he who opens wide his lips shall have destruction."*

If you continue to utter that you are sick and tired, guess what you are going to be? Sick and tired. If you say over and over that you are poor, you are going to be poor by the accursed words of your own mouth. If you continually whine and declare negative statements over yourself such as, "Nobody likes me," you are going to be friendless.

The words we speak are a vital component to our healing. They either allow the healing to manifest or they prevent the power of God to produce a miracle. If you desire healing you must speak words that are full of life and healing.

We must learn to put a guard on our mouth and think before we speak.

BLESSING AND CURSING PROCEED FROM THE SAME MOUTH

James shares great wisdom about the power of the tongue; let's turn to James 3:9-10. *"With it we bless our God and Father, and with it we curse men, who have been made in the similitude of God. Out of the same mouth proceed blessing and cursing. My brethren, these things ought not to be so."* It's disgraceful to hear ourselves praise the Lord with our words and immediately turn to those around us and hurl insults or words of discouragement at them. It's like we are driving around in a bulldozer and the nearest person in our path gets bulldozed over by our words of insult or discouragement, and then we stop for a while to have a praise moment, as if we were on a coffee break, and then continue on. The Word of God is clear—this should not be.

Just because we think someone is weaker than we are or they have a physical flaw does not give us the right to pick them apart. We are all made in the image of God, and when we insult another person we actually insult God.

There is the old cliché that says, "Sticks and stones may break our bones, but words will never hurt us." This is a lie; it's unbiblical. A physical wound usually heals much quicker than a verbal one. So let's think twice before we wag our tongues so loosely.

VERBAL CLAIM TO SICKNESS AND DISEASE

With the power of words that proceed from our own mouths we take ownership of sickness and disease when we declare that it belongs to us. When we make declarations such as, "My cancer is back, my diabetes is acting up, my arthritis is bothering me" with the usage of possessive pronouns—*my* and *our*—we make a verbal claim that this wicked work of satan belongs to us. We bind ourselves to it; we create a spiritual tie to it. In doing so, we give the illness the verbal okay to stay, dominate, and subdue us. Even with every moan and complaint we utter about it, we give it strength.

NEGATIVE WORD LABELS

It takes an intervention of the Holy Spirit to overcome a negative word label. Gabriel gave Mary a word of knowledge in Luke 1:36 concerning her cousin Elizabeth. He says, *"And behold, even your relative Elizabeth has also conceived a son in her old age; and she who was called barren is now in her sixth month"* (NASB).

In the natural it was impossible for Elizabeth to conceive a child. She was labeled *barren*. The Common English Bible reads, *"Look, even in her old age, your relative Elizabeth has conceived a son. This woman who was labeled 'unable to conceive' is now six months pregnant."* Her womb was labeled with the words *forever empty* and *childless*.

God is the Master at overriding natural impossibilities and transforming them into possibilities. He removes negative word labels that bind people to hopelessness and despair. He confirms this in Luke 1:37, *"For with God nothing [is or ever] shall be impossible"* (AMP).

My husband, before I knew him, was labeled as an alcoholic and a drug addict in his teenage years. It was a generational curse passed down from his father. A high school teacher recognized the signs and reached out to him, and he was enrolled in a local AA program. They helped him immensely, but he lived with the fear of the label—once an alcoholic, always an alcoholic.

I met him several years later, and on our first date I invited him to come to church with me. It was a new experience for him to be in the presence of the Lord. The message of the Lord pierced his heart that morning, and when the altar call was given he knelt down before thousands of people and gave his life to Christ and became born again. The revelation of Second Corinthians 5:17 that was spoken out that from the pulpit resonated within his spirit, and he knew in his heart and even vocalized the fact that he no longer was an alcoholic or drug addict. He walked free from the power of those labels and never returned to those old temptations.

> *Therefore if anyone is in Christ [that is, grafted in, joined to Him by faith in Him as Savior], he is a new creature [reborn and renewed by the Holy Spirit]; the old things [the previous moral and spiritual condition] have passed away. Behold, new things have come [because spiritual awakening brings a new life]* (2 Corinthians 5:17 AMP).

What physical impossibility have you been labeled with? Is there an underlying hope within you to be free from the stronghold of this negative label? This hope is the precursor to faith to believe and receive your miracle from God today. Hebrews puts it this way:

> *Now faith is the assurance (title deed, confirmation) of things hoped for (divinely guaranteed), and the evidence of things not seen [the*

conviction of their reality—faith comprehends as fact what cannot be experienced by the physical senses] (Hebrews 11:1 AMP).

Spiritually prepare your heart to receive. Just like a womb receives a miracle seed to produce life, you receive this message as your hope seed and witness the label *impossible* transform into *possible*. You start right now and take the supernatural power of the word *impossible* or the negative report, vocally renounce the situation in the name of Jesus, and transform it and say with God aloud, "This too is possible!"

Ask Anything in His Name

His Word promises us in John 14:14 *"If you ask anything in My name, I will do it."* What an amazing promise this is to us. It's limitless, like our God. What is it that you have need of? He is faithful to perform His Word, and if you believe you will receive what you ask of Him.

What do you have need of? Do you need a new kidney? Vocalize your need, and ask Him for one.

Dear Father God,

I ask you for a new kidney that functions perfectly normally. I believe and I receive it right now by faith.

In Jesus' name, amen.

Whether you need a new kidney or something else, ask the Father in Jesus' name and He will give it to you.

Ask with Confidence

Some members of the body of Christ believe it is presumptuous of us to believe this way; others claim we are like dictators ordering our Lord around, but the truth is that He desires us to be well-informed of His will and to have confidence in our faith in Him. Faith pleases Him, and it gives Him great pleasure when we are bold in our faith.

Because we know what we ask for is found in the will of God—such as eternal life, healing, deliverance, protection, and daily provision—we can be confident in our faith and ask Him for what we have need of. John educates us in how we are to ask:

> *Now this is the confidence that we have in Him, that if we ask anything according to His will, He hears us. And if we know that He hears us, whatever we ask, we know that we have the petitions that we have asked of Him* (1 John 5:14-15).

ADDRESSING THE ABUSE OF THIS PRINCIPLE

I know there are many who have abused this principle, but this doesn't mean that we throw the baby out with the bathwater. The abuse that is commonly used is that they ask amiss. The motives of their heart are evil, selfish, irresponsible, and greedy. We do not have to submit ourselves to their ungodliness.

You wonder, "If their motives are wrong, then why do they still receive?" Because they are activating the power of the spoken word that is given to all people, believers or unbelievers. This includes believers with wrong motives. Judgement will come upon them for their sins. We do not need to take up this concern. It's between them and God. My part is to make sure I am not caught up in their greed.

It's the righteousness of God within us to ask our Lord for healings, miracles, daily provisions, etc. We honor Him when we ask in faith for the things He promises to give us. It proves that we take Him at His word. We believe.

SPEAK LIFE AND DEATH
ACCORDING TO THE NEED

We need to be wise in the way we speak words of life and death. We need to vocalize the power of our words according to the need of the situation.

If we are in a battle against heart disease, we first ask in faith for a new heart. We do not beg and plead as if God is evil and withholds healing from us. Then we use the Sword of the Spirit, and we grow the miracle. We speak words of faith to that which we have need of.

In Jesus' name, I renounce the spirit of premature death; I release the power of the Holy Spirit into my heart. I command my heart to be healed, to be recreated, to function perfectly normally. I demand all sickness and disease, pain and swelling to be gone. I declare my heart healed and made whole in Jesus' name.

Our words have the power of life and death, so we are to destroy the effects of premature death and create life into our heart—actually, speak life into it. Then we put our faith into action and act out what we say we believe for. In other words, if we desire a new heart, then we start to plan our future to live with a new heart. We plan tomorrow, the next week, and next year to live with a new heart.

Thus also faith by itself, if it does not have works, is dead (James 2:17).

With Your Voice Exercise Authority over Satan

As we discussed in Chapter 5, we hold the authority of Christ and can subdue the devil. One of the main ways we accomplish this is by the power of the spoken word. We dominate him and his wicked works, including sickness and disease, as we adjure him to stop in the name of Jesus and renounce the workings of his wickedness—all with the backing of the blood of Christ Jesus.

When we adjure the devil, we command him, we take charge over him, we bind up his efforts in the name of the Lord. For example, "We adjure you, satan, to leave and take this cancer with you in Jesus' name!" "We adjure you, devil, we take charge over you and command you to get out of our household and stop this harassment at once in Jesus' name!" "We adjure you, foul wicked spirit, we bind you up to the effects of your own wickedness! You will not have your way in this body, in Jesus' name!" As you notice, we do not beg, we do not plead, and we do not give him opportunity to talk back. We certainly do not enter into a conversation with him!

Curse Sickness

God gives you His blessing to curse satan and his wicked works, including sickness and disease. So right now, obey His Word and curse this illness at its very root and seed, just like Jesus cursed the fig tree (see Mark 11:12–25).

Use the Sword of the Spirit; go down deep into the root system and cut this disease off of your body. Curse the tap root and command it to dry up and die, and all other roots that stem off of this main root dry up and disappear supernaturally. Remind it often that it will not be able to resurrect itself in your body. Nor can it transplant or metastasize itself in any other part of your body.

Speak to the original seed of this disease, the seed of sin that was planted back in the Garden of Eden when Adam and Eve first sinned. Renounce this generational curse because you have been redeemed from it (see Gal. 3:13).

Dominate all seeds that this disease has produced to wither and die. Put them in their place beneath your authority in Jesus Christ; let them know who is boss and that they may not germinate ever again in your body or pass on to another generation.

Vocalize Creation

There is a right way to use the power of the spoken word, and it not only destroys the wicked works of satan, like sickness and disease, but it creates healings and miracles for those in need.

In chapter 1 of Genesis we read the historical account of how our Creator, Elohim, creates all of creation with the power of the spoken word.

He said, "Let there be," and there was. Then He created the human race in His mirror image, and we too inherit the power of the spoken word.

CREATE AN ATMOSPHERE OF HEALING

Wherever you are going, see yourself walking in His sandals of authority, knowing that even before arriving He's already giving you this territory and you going there is glorifying the Lord.

Joshua 1:3 declares, *"Every place that the sole of your foot will tread upon I have given you, as I said to Moses."*

Before you walk into a hospital, be vocal, pray the Spirit of the Lord into that place, and thank Him in advance that His miracle power will work through you and the people who will accept your healing hands will be healed in Jesus' name.

When you speak out words of faith before you minister, you till up the hard ground, you weed out doubt and unbelief, you seed healing, you water and nurture it. When you go into that hospital, you reap the harvest of the garden you plant.

I already hear some of you say, "Sister Becky, we can't do that in our country." Do you not hear what the Spirit of the Lord says to you?

> *If My people who are called by My name will humble themselves, and pray and seek My face, and turn from their wicked ways, then I will hear from heaven, and will forgive their sin and heal their land* (2 Chronicles 7:14).

Dear servants of the Lord, let me ask you a pertinent question, "Where does it say in the Word that we will not run into opposition as we do the work of the Lord?" Nowhere! In fact we read the opposite—from the time Jesus was born, even while He was still in the womb, everywhere that He went opposition followed. It didn't matter if He was in the temple, outside the temple, in the city, His hometown, the countryside, in a private residence, or out in the open, He was met by great opposition by the Pharisees and the Sadducees, the rulers in government, unbelievers, and the devil himself was out to stop Him. But they could not. Why? He went up to the mountaintop and got vocal and interceded on the behalf of the people.

Get down on your knees and, with vocal prayer, pray in the Spirit and declare with your native tongue words of faith that will create the atmosphere of healing that you need in your territory for the glory of our Lord.

No Disease Will Prosper in My Body

I have a weapon of mass destruction—the blood of Jesus Christ that obviates, literally wipes from existence, every sickness and disease, known or unknown, that would try to enter into my physical body. I own a copy of the map of the battlefield, and on Calvary Hill the battle has been won. The battle plan in Isaiah 54:17 assures me *"No weapon formed against you shall prosper."*

When God's Word declares that satan's dirty bombs of sickness and disease cannot prosper against me, it means they have transformed into duds. They cannot succeed in their plan to kill me. They do not even have the right to thrive in my human body. They've crossed the line, and they must leave in Jesus' name.

With the strength of the spoken word, I build a supernatural defense system around me that deflects the weaponry of the devil.

When I Am Weak, He Remains Strong

Our Lord is not uncaring; He understands what we are up against. Hebrews 4:15 identifies the reason why, *"For we do not have a High Priest who cannot sympathize with our weaknesses, but was in all points tempted as we are, yet without sin."*

His healing word declares that when I am weak, He remains strong in me (see 2 Cor. 12:10). Isaiah 40:29 affirms this promise, *"He gives power to the weak, and to those who have no might He increases strength."* Zechariah 4:6 educates me on how this is possible, *"'Not by might nor by power, but by My Spirit,' says the Lord of hosts."* He assures me in Philippians 4:13 that

"I can do all things through Christ who strengthens me." I can overcome this seemingly impossible moment in my life and heal too in Jesus' name.

BOLDLY DECLARE

When the attack of the enemy bears down hard and the reports shout death, I will not fear. I put my trust in my God:

> *Now to Him who is able to do exceedingly abundantly above all that we ask or think, according to the power that works in us, to Him be glory in the church by Christ Jesus to all generations, forever and ever. Amen* (Ephesians 3:20-21).

Like Abraham, I too believe *"in the presence of Him whom he believed—God, who gives life to the dead and calls those things which do not exist as though they did"* (Rom. 4:17). I boldly declare His abundant life, healing power, and supernatural strength to overtake my body.

I bind myself to the power of the blood of Jesus to take down this illness, to heal me, to recreate this physical body of mine, to renew my strength. According to the healing words of Isaiah 40:29–31, because I wait upon the Lord, I will mount up with wings like eagles, I will run and not be weary, I will walk and not faint, in Jesus' name I declare, amen.

IN JESUS' NAME

The Healing Creed ends with "in Jesus' name." This phrase is not a religious tagline but a supernatural seal to the message of the creed that we declare aloud. The seal behind the name of Jesus is the power of His shed blood.

The Book of John teaches us the importance of ending our prayers in the name of Jesus. Yes, our confessions of faith are prayers. Prayers are made up of words that we confess.

The healing power of the redemptive blood of Jesus Christ is the foundation for the Healing Creed. As we verbalize this scriptural creed, we release

God's creative healing power over our bodies. I suggest we confess this faith document for healing over our bodies three times a day in Jesus' name.

Romans 10:9 says, *"If you confess with your mouth the Lord Jesus and believe in your heart that God has raised Him from the dead, you will be saved."* Remember what we learned in Chapter 3 about the word *saved*? It comes from the Greek word *sōzō* and means to save, deliver, protect, heal, preserve, save, do well, and to be made whole.

"For with the heart one believes unto righteousness, and with the mouth confession is made unto salvation" (Rom. 10:10). By our verbal confession we activate the power of salvation, and in this work we release the healing power of salvation.

It is scriptural to pray in Jesus' name. Below, are six scriptures from the Book of John that confirm we are to pray in His name and teach us the benefit when we do so.

> *And whatever you ask in My name, that I will do, that the Father may be glorified in the Son* (John 14:13).

> *If you ask anything in My name, I will do it* (John 14:14).

> *You did not choose Me, but I chose you and appointed you that you should go and bear fruit, and that your fruit should remain, that whatever you ask the Father in My name He may give you* (John 15:16).

> *And in that day you will ask Me nothing. Most assuredly, I say to you, whatever you ask the Father in My name He will give you* (John 16:23).

> *Until now you have asked nothing in My name. Ask, and you will receive, that your joy may be full* (John 16:24).

> *In that day you will ask in My name, and I do not say to you that I shall pray the Father for you* (John 16:26).

These scriptures are clear in the spiritual correctness of prayer. If we ask anything, whatever we ask, we are to ask the Father in the name of Jesus or we ask Jesus directly. However we make our needs or desires known through prayer, we are always to go through the avenue of Jesus' name. He explains to His disciples, and we are His modern-day disciples, that if we ask in His name, He will do it. If we ask the Father in the name of Jesus, the Father will do it.

This isn't about being religious but being obedient and giving recognition to whom it is due. Jesus paid the price with His blood so that we can have His benefits, such as healing. There is a protocol when we ask, pray, or verbally confess with our mouths, and it is through the spiritual bloodline of Jesus' name.

HEALING TESTIMONY: ULCERATIVE COLITIS HEALED

After a year of mild bleeding, Yolanda from Purcellville, Virginia was diagnosed with moderate to severe ulcerative colitis in 2014, but that summer she had a severe flare of over 40 bloody bowel movements a day (just blood), severe anemia, and dehydration.

She suffered from severe pain, cramping, tunnel vision, loss of hearing, and sensitivity to sound. She was unable to eat without pain, and could only tolerate eggs, zucchini, ground beef, protein shakes, and herbs. She tried all sorts of home remedies without results. She went from 125 pounds down to 95 pounds. She was so weak that she was not able to get out of bed for seven weeks. Her friends who came to visit later told her that they thought she was not going to survive. From a natural standpoint, they were right.

As difficult as this battle was, she did not give up. She read my first work, watched videos, and learned how the enemy is under her authority and how he flees at the name of Jesus.

After fasting months earlier, she felt the Lord say to her, "Pray believing." But then her question was, "Believe what?" She hadn't really thought about that and assumed it was believe that Jesus is who He says He is, but later she realized the part that was missing for her was that He loved her just like He says He does. This was harder for her to accept than the fact He willed to heal her.

Nevertheless, she asked the Lord to heal her. She heard the Lord respond to her request. Let's listen to Yolanda share this part of her story.

> The Lord had given me a word, which was, "I will not condemn those whose faith is in me." I believed He was going to heal me.
>
> But after seven weeks of the flare and none of the symptoms improving, my husband wanted me to go to the gastroenterologist. The doctor told us that I was not going to recover without a heavy dose of steroids and biologics, which are known to cause cancer. I reluctantly agreed that I would begin the next morning.
>
> But that night Chris and I prayed together. I remember I confessed an issue of pride that I struggled with, and told God that I believed that He would heal me and take care of me, whether I took the medications or not. And I was overwhelmed when the Holy Spirit took over my mouth, and I prayed in tongues.
>
> That night, several times I felt someone's breath on my ear as I slept, and I thought it was one my children, but every time I looked no one was there.
>
> Then I heard the Lord say to me, "Do not take the drugs; I have something else for you." The next morning I woke up healed. And that was confirmed by how wonderful I felt! I was able to go down the stairs, clean the kitchen, and make it back up the stairs as if I had not been anemic or dehydrated.

At this time, Yolanda was unaware of how much satan hates to see God's people heal and that he was not about to walk away without a fight. Perhaps he could still convince her to doubt God's promise to heal her. Let's listen to what she has to say about this again.

I did not know that the enemy would try to steal my healing from me, so I did not claim what the Lord had provided for me. But, in time, I learned how to believe and possess my healing.

What I feel made the difference was when I finally reached a point where I trusted the Lord no matter what. During all of this, the Lord worked something out in my husband and me and the others to trust Him even when the symptoms and doctor said there was no hope.

At times, I would get a cramp but realized it was an opportunity to solidify what I believed. So I would cry out loud, "Jesus is Lord!" and it would immediately go away. I have been free from cramps for a very long time now.

The Lord has restored my family and my marriage, renewed my husband's spiritual walk, encouraged the doctor, surrounded us with wonderful people, and gave us rest.

What a beautiful testimony of God's patience and faithfulness to work with His people, not against them, like many believe, until Yolanda was able to come to the spiritual place where she put her trust in Jesus and was healed.

In order for Yolanda and her family to overcome satan, the spirit of fear, and the spirit of death, they had to first believe in the power of the blood of Christ to heal, then they had to wield their supernatural Sword of the Spirit with authority and grace. They had to learn how to guard their tongues and speak life, no matter what was manifesting from her body.

As they did, she mounted up with wings like eagles, she ran and was not weary, and she walked and did not faint—out of the Valley of the Shadow of Death and into the Promised Land where miracles grow.

PRAYER

Dear Father God,

We are now well-informed about Your will to heal us. With confidence we voice activate Your creative healing power within us.

Teach us, Holy Spirit, to wield this supernatural weapon, the Sword of the Spirit, effectively. Remind us to control the power of our words—that yes, there indeed is the power of life and death in our tongues. Forgive us for speaking such negative and faithless words in the past.

Lead us as we create victory out of the chaos of life by speaking faith-filled words that will glorify our Father in Heaven.

We renounce the verbal claims that we have made to sickness and disease. We've cursed ourselves and others by the daily usage of worldly labels. Forgive us for this.

We verbalize our God-given authority over satan and all of his wicked works, including sickness and disease. We adjure him, command him in the name of Jesus to leave our households, to flee our physical bodies in Jesus' name.

We curse this sickness from its very root and seed and declare by faith that our bodies are disease-free.

We thank You that when our physical bodies are weak, You remain strong in us.

We boldly declare Your abundant life, Your healing power, and Your supernatural strength to overtake our physical bodies.

We bind ourselves to the power of the blood of Jesus to take down this illness, to heal us, to recreate these physical bodies of ours, and to renew our strength.

We understand that there is a spiritual correctness to our prayer language, and from now on we ask, we pray, we verbalize our confession of faith through the spiritual bloodline of Jesus' name.

In Jesus' name we pray, amen.

✝

SELF-EXAMINATION

Do I understand my spiritual weapon, the Sword of the Spirit? Am I willing to repent for misusing the power of my words? Am I willing to change my vocabulary to destroy the power of satan and his wicked works, including sickness and disease, and verbally create healing and miracles that will not only benefit myself but others around me? With prayers of faith-filled words, will I create an atmosphere conducive to healing? Has the Holy Spirit revealed to me a specific place or a person I need to take the message of healing to? Do I pray in the name of Jesus? If not, will I start to pray in His name today?

ABOUT BECKY DVORAK

✝

Becky Dvorak, author of *Dare to Believe* and *Greater Than Magic*, content partner with Spirit Led Woman/Charisma, is a prophetic healing evangelist and conducts healing services, seminars, and conferences globally. Along with her husband, David, they have been full-time missionaries since 1994 in Guatemala, Central America and founders of Healing and Miracles International and Vida Ilimitada. They celebrate thirty-six years of marriage and have eight children—three adult biological and five adopted—and seven grandchildren.

Made in the USA
Lexington, KY
05 May 2019